The Farmyard Companion

Cows are my passion.

from *Dombey and Son*
Charles Dickens (1812–70)

A member of the Women's Land Army –
all in a day's work! May 1918

The Farmyard Companion

compiled by Peter Isaac

Jill Norman & Hobhouse

Thank goodness I have friends! Without
them, this miscellany would never have been
completed. Rosemary Oxley, who designed the
book, must have been driven nearly out of her
mind by my vagueness. Jane Poynor has proved
a never ending source of sensible advice and
tireless research. Mike Reynolds gave
invaluable advice and suggestions, as well as
encouragement. Denis Coggins, of the Bowes
Museum, went to untold trouble on my behalf,
as did Dr S. Ward, of the Museum of English
Rural Life, in Reading. Caroline Parton of
Punch, Mary Evans of the Mary Evans Picture
Library and Mr and Mrs Stone of Titles, in
Oxfordshire, have all gone out of their way
to help. I am indebted to Lawrence Alderson
of the Rare Breeds Survival Trust for his advice
and statistics on farm animals in Great Britain.
Many other friends and aquaintances, too
numerous to mention, gave valuable help and
guidance. Finally, I would like to thank my
publisher Jill Norman and her editor Emma
Johnson for putting up with my endless
queries, and still having faith to proceed
with the book.

Peter Isaac 1981

Jill Norman & Hobhouse Ltd
90 Great Russell Street
London WC1B 3PY

Published by Jill Norman & Hobhouse 1981
Copyright ©Peter Isaac 1981

British Library Cataloguing in Publication Data

The farmyard companion
   1. English poetry (Collections)
   I. Isaac, Peter
   821'.008'36   PR1195.F/

ISBN 0-906908-51-5

Designed by Rosemary Oxley
Art Editor Ray Carpenter
Research Jane Poynor
Typeset by V & M Graphics Ltd, Aylesbury, Bucks
Printed and bound in Great Britain
by Richard Clay Ltd, Bungay, Suffolk

Belonging to the Arrable and Field-Land, are

Harrows.
Forkes.
Sickles.
Reap-hooks.
Weed-hooks.
Pitchforks.
Rakes.
Plough-ftaff and Beetle.
Sledds.
Roller.
Mold-fpears and Traps.
Cradle-fythes.
Seed-lip.

Yoakes for Oxen.
Pannnels.
Wanteyes.
Pack-faddles.
Suffingles.
Cart-lines.
Skrein for Corn.

To Meadows and Paftures.
Sythes.
Rakes.
Pitchforks and Prongs.
Fetters and Clogs and Shackles.
Cutting Spade for Hay-reeks.
Horfe locks.

Other neceffary Inftruments.
Hand barrows.
Wheel barrows.
Dibbles.
Hammer and Nails.

To the Barn and Stable

Flayles.
Ladders.
Winnowing-fan.
Meafures for Corn.
Sieves and Rudders.
Broomes.
Sacks.
Skeps or Scuttles.
Bins.
Payles.
Curry-combs.
Main-combs.
Whips.
Goads.
Harneys for Horfes, and Yoaks

Pincers.
Siffers.
Bridle and Saddle.
Nail-piercers or Gimlets.
Hedging-hooks and Bills.
Garden-fheers.
A Grindftone.
Whetftones.
Hatchets and Axes.
Sawes.
Beetle and Wedges.
Leavers.
Shears for Sheep.
Trowels for Houfe and Garden
Hodd and Tray.
Hog-Yoaks and Rings.
Marks for Beafts and Utenfils.
Scales and Weights.
An Aul, and every other thing neceffary.

Equipment suggested by John Worlidge for the farm in the seventeenth century.

Polish peasant resting in market place, Lodz.

Introduction

In these pages I have assembled a pot pourri of farmyard-inspired writings, photographs, and other illustrations. I found the material fascinating not only for its intrinsic charm and humour, but also as an indication of ways of life which are now largely of the past.

When I was three, I spent a short but wonderful holiday in the country and ever since I have enjoyed whatever time I spent on farms. Sadly, the individual character of farms and their inhabitants is fast disappearing as farming becomes more streamlined. A four thousand pig-growing unit does not create the kind of atmosphere we attribute to the old mixed farmyard where everyone in the family had a job and where the livestock formed a separate but closely related community.

Although through the centuries country people have often suffered great poverty and deprivation, they have at the same time developed a sense of independence, a personal pride, and often a great sense of humour. The struggle to survive from year to year, constantly at the mercy of nature, never certain if rain or drought would not ruin the next crop or disease wipe out livestock, destroying a lifetime's work of breeding and cross-breeding, developed people of remarkable resilience, with skills and a particular kind of wisdom too often ignored, dismissed or ridiculed by townsfolk.

Of course, the farmyard as a mini empire with its monarchs, peers and serfs has always been an ideal source for all forms of satire, with the extremes of self-indulgence personified by the pig, placid resignation by the cow, stupidity by sheep and lamb, neurosis by the chicken, matronliness by the duck, empty-headed arrogance by the turkey, general unfriendliness by the goose, and dependable reliability by the horse. By creating these stereotyped images the people of town and city may have asserted their air of superiority, but at the same time they lost the ability to see things as they really were.

The sequence in which I have arranged the material is simply chronological, but where the odd entry seemed to fit a theme rather than a time I have cheated. This should not cause too much confusion, since as far as possible dates have been included for authors and sources.

THE KINDELY PROPERTIE OF EVERY MONTH

January	A kindely good Janiuere, freaseth potte by the fier.
February	Fill (Feuerill) dike, with what thou dost like.
Marche	Marche dust to be solde, worth raunsomes of golde.
April	Swete Aprill showers, do spring the May flowers.
May	Colde May and a windy makes Barns fat and findy.
June	Calme weather in June, corne setteth in tune.
July	No tempest good Julye, least al things looke ruly.
August	Dry August and warme, doth harvest no harme.
September	September blowe softe, till fruite be in lofte.
October	October good blast, to shake the Hog mast.
November	November take flaile, let Ship no more saile.
December	Oh dirtye December, for Christmas remember.

Thomas Tusser, 1571

Flemish Book of Hours, c. 1500

Butter is made of crayme . . . it is good to eate in the mornyng before other meates . . . a lytell porcyon is good for every man in the morenynge if it be newe made.

Of all thynges let the buttery, the cellar, the kytchen, the larder house, with all other howses of offyces, be kept clene, that there be no fylth in them, but good odyferous savours.

Thomas Tusser (1524?–80)

Milking in the field and butter churning:
German, sixteenth century

9

MARKHAMS
Maister Peece.
Containing all knowledge
belonging to Smith Farrier, or
Horse leech. touching the
curing of all diseases
in Horses.
Deuided into two bookes
The first. containing all
cures Physicall.
The second all belonging
to Chyrurgery.
The 11.th Impression corrected
and enlarged by the Author.
Geruase Markham.

To which is now added
The Country mans Care
For Curing Diseases in
Smaller Cattle.

Ren Elstrak sculpsit

In 1683, Gervase Markham wrote his 'Master-piece' which dealt with all the diseases in horses. He included in later editions an appendix on 'The Country-man's Care' for all diseases of oxen, cows, sheep, hogs, goats, and all small 'cattel'. In Markham's day, the blacksmith was also the horse doctor, hence the illustration opposite of the farrier's art.

The Mind or Meaning of the FRONTISPIECE.

THe Figure 1. a compleat *Horseman* shows,
  That *Rides, Keeps, Cures,* and all perfections knows.
The 2. *Diet*; the 3. Letting Blood,
Best *Balm* of *Balms,* for inward Griefs most good:
The 4. *Wounds, Galls,* and *Sores* doth firmly cure;
The 5. helps *Natures* Marks ; 6. doth procure
Help for the *Sinews* Griefs, as *Slip* or *Strain,*
Knock, or *Convulsion,* all are helpt again.
The 7. wholsom *Drink* ; the 8 doth take
Blood from the *Mouth,* which sudden Death doth slake.
The 9. shews the *Horse-Caudle,* or the *Mash,*
Good as the best, yet some Fools count it Trash.
The 10. shews *Fury* in untamed things,
The only *Fountain* whence *Diseases* springs.

November: Gathering Acorns for Pigs
From the Calendar of the Playfair Book of Hours,
late 15th century

Though plenty of acorns, the porkling to fat
not taken in season, may perish by that:
If rattling or swelling, get once to the throat,
thou losest thy porkling, a crown to a groat.

from *Five Hundred Good Points of Husbandry*, 1571
Thomas Tusser

December: Slaughtering Pigs
From the Calendar of the Playfair Book of Hours,
late 15th century

At Hallontide, slaughter-time entereth in,
and then doth the husbandman's feasting begin:
From thence unto Shrovetide, kill now and then some,
their offall for household the better will come.

from *Five Hundred Good Points of Husbandry*, 1571
Thomas Tusser

'E KILLING O' 'E PEEG

Weel fed id hed been for a while,
  an' treated lek a freen,
But 'e time hed come for slaughter
  on 'at very aifterneen;
'E owld man's han' wis steady,
  his blade wis sharp an' keen;
'E peeg, id squealed a bitty
  fan couped heels abeen;
'E deed wis swiftly cairried oot
  afore yer very een;
An' 'e bleed wis catched for puddens
  in 'e owld wife's muckle tureen.

Geddes O'Mey, 1978

Ploughing; taken from an Anglo-Saxon manuscript

OXEN V. HORSE

The horse costs more than the ox ... besides a
plough of oxen will go as far in the year as a
plough of horses because the malice of ploughmen will not allow the plough to go beyond their
face, no more than the plough of oxen. Further
in very hard ground where the plough of horses
will stop the plough of oxen will pass ... and it is
usual and right that plough beasts should be in
the stall between the feast of St. Luke and the
feast of the Holy Cross in May 25 weeks, it is
necessary that he should have every night at least
the 6th part of a bushel of oats price 1 half
penny and at the least 12 penny-worth of grass
in summer and each week more or less a penny
in shoeing if he must be shod on all four feet ...
If the ox is to be in condition to do his work,
then it is necessary that he should have at least 3
sheaves and a half of oats in the week, price one
penny ... and when the horse is old and worn
out then there is nothing but the skin; and when
the ox is old with tenpennyworth of grass he
shall be fit for the larder.

Thomas Tusser, 1571

14

Medieval England; *Cosmographie Universalis*
1553, Sebastian Munster

I HAVE TWELVE OXEN

I have twelve oxen that be fair and brown,
And they go a-grazing down by the town.
With hay, with howe, with hay!
Sawest thou not mine oxen, thou litill pretty boy.

I have twelve oxen and they be fair and white,
And they go a-grazing down by the dyke.
With hay, with howe, with hay!
Sawest thou not mine oxen, thou litill pretty boy.

I have twelve oxen and they be fair and blak,
And they go a-grazing down by the lak.
With hay, with howe, with hay!
Sawest thou not mine oxen, thou litill pretty boy.

I have twelve oxen and they be faire and rede,
And they go a-grazing down by the mede.
With hay, with howe, with hay!
Sawest thou not mine oxen, thou litill pretty boy.

Robbins, 15th century

The Domestic Cock:
woodcut by **Thomas Bewick** (1753–1828)

She had a yard that was enclosed about
By a stockade and a dry ditch without,
In which she kept a cock called Chanticleer.
In all the land for crowing he'd no peer;
His voice was jollier than the organ blowing
In church on Sundays, he was great at crowing.
Far, far more regular than any clock
Or abbey bell the crowing of this cock.
The equinoctial wheel and its position
At each ascent he knew by intuition;
At every hour – fifteen degrees of movement –
He crowed so well there could be
   no improvement.
His comb was redder than fine coral, tall
And battlemented like a castle wall,
His bill was black and shone as bright as jet,
Like azure were his legs and they were set
On azure toes with nails of lily white,
Like burnished gold his feathers,
   flaming bright.

from *The Nun's Priest's Tale: The Canterbury Tales*
Geoffrey Chaucer (1340?–1400);
translated by Nevill Coghill

The chickens are the countrys, but the city
eats them.

George Herbert (1593–1633)

I want there to be no peasant in my kitchen so
poor that he is unable to have a chicken in
his pot every Sunday.

Hardouin de Beaumont de Péréfixe (1605–71)

If Cocks crow more than ordinary, especially
in the evening, or if Poultrey go early to
roost, it signifies Rain.

Prognosticks, 1669, **John Worlidge**

While the cock with lively din,
Scatters the rear of darkness thin,
And to the stack, or the barn door,
Stoutly struts his dames before.

from *L'Allegro*
John Milton (1608–74)

Rammes. To increase their lusts ... give them ... in their pasture the blades of Onions, or knot Grasse: also their blossoming in the North wind getteth Ramme Lambes, and in the South winde ewe Lambes, one Ramme (as Didymus affirmeth) sufficeth for 50 ewes.

from *Five Hundred Good Points of Husbandry*, 1571
Thomas Tusser

If Sheep feed more than ordinary, it signifies Rain, or if the Rams skip up and down, and eat greedily.

Prognosticks, 1669, **John Worlidge**

From the *Luttrell Psalter*, 14th century

THE FARMER'S FEAST DAYS

God huswives who God hath enriched enough
forget not the feasts that belong to the Plough,
The meaning is onely to joy and be glad,
for comfort with labour whould sometimes be had.

Plough Munday

Plough Munday, the next after Twelftide be past,
biddeth out with the plough, the worst husband is last.
If Ploughman get hatchet or whip to the skreene,
maydes loseth their Cocke if no Water be seene.

Shrovetide

At Shrovetide to shroving go thresh the fatte henne,
if blindefilde can kill it then geve it thy menne.
Maides fritters and panckes inough see ye make,
let slutte have one pancake for company sake.

Sheepshearing

Wife make us a feast, spare fleshe neither corne,
make Wafers and cakes, for our shepe must be shorne.
At sheep shearing neighbours no other thing crave
but good chere and welcome like neighbours to have.

The Wake Day

To Oven with the flawns mayd, passe not for slepe,
to-morrow thy father his wake day shal kepe;
Then trimly go daunce with what Lover ye will,
though love make you beaten, kepe Lover yet still.

Harvest Home

For all this good feasting yet art thou not loose
till thou geve the Ploughman in harvest his goose.
Though goose go in stubble, yet passe not for that,
let goose have a goose be shee leane be shee fat.

Seed Cake

Wife, sometime this weeke if that all thing go cleare,
and ende of wheat sowing we make for this yeare,
Remember you therefore though I do it not
the Seede Cake, the Pasties, and Furmenty pot.

Twice a Weke Rost

Good Ploughman looke wekely of custome and right

for rostmeat and Sundaies and Thursdaies at night:
Thus doing and keeping such custome and guise,
they call thee good huswife, they love thee likewise.

CHRISTMAS HUSBANDLY FARE

Good Husband and Huswife, now chiefly be glad,
things handsome to have, as they ought to be had.
They both do provide, against Christmas do come,
to welcom their neighbors, good chere to have some.

Good bread and good drinke, a good fier in the hall,
brawne, pudding, and souse, and good mustarde withal.
Biefe, mutton, and Porke, and good Pies of the best,
pig, veale, goose, and capon, and turkey wel drest,
Chese, apples, and nuttes, and good Caroles to heare,
as then, in the cuntrey is counted good cheare.

What cost to good husbande, is any of this?
good housholde provision onely it is:
Of other the like, I do leave out a meny,
that costeth the husband never a peny.

Thomas Tusser, 1571

From the *Luttrell Psalter*, 14th century

Frontispiece from *The Book of Husbandry*,
1534, Master Fitzherbert

The following are extracts from Gervase Markham's
Master-piece, 1683

The right Method for the Ordering of Cattel.

I. Of OXEN.

THE worthy Author having excellently treated of the Order and Government of Horſes, both as to their Breeding, Feeding and managing, as alſo for the Curing of all Diſeaſes they are, or may be incident to, I thought it very proper to add by way of *Appendix*, this ſhort, but neceſſary Treatiſe for the direction of the painful Country-man in his ordering all other ſorts of Cattel, *viz.* Oxen, Cows, Sheep, Hogs, *&c.* and herein i ſhall be as ſhort as may be, giving you only thoſe approved Receits, which not only the former, but theſe modern times have frequently experienced.

CHAP. I.

For the Cough in Oxen.

A Cough of no long continuance may ſoon be remedied by a Drink which you make with Water and Barley-Meal, adding ſome Bean-Flower and ſome Stich-wort and ſo given to your Beaſt.

A certain Cure for an old Cough, is to ſteep two pound of Hyſſop in a quart or two of Water, well mixt with eight Pounds of Lentil-peaſe mingled together; Likewiſe give the Beaſt fine Wheat and Roots of Leeks clean waſhed, well beat together, faſting. You may alſo ſtamp Garlick with Dragon-Water, new Ale and Butter, and being warm give it the Beaſt.

For a Beaſt's Hoof hurt.

IF your Ox by chance be hurt with a Stub of Wood, or with a Coulter or Share, or any part of the Clees, mix but the Powder of Brimſtone with a Salve of Pitch and old Greaſe well melted together; then pour it hot on any ſore part.

To keep your Beaſts from Foundring, when you unyoke them, waſh their Feet with cold Water, likewiſe let their Paſterns and Clees be anointed with old Greaſe, and they will do well.

To cure the Gravel or a Cut in an Oxes foot, let him be bathed in warm Water, then melt Tar and old Greaſe for an Ointment, and if with old freſh Greaſe you rub and chafe his Feet, before you unyoke them, nothing is better to preſerve them.

CHAP. III.

For a Bruiſe on a Beaſt's Shoulder.

Labouring Oxen may be lame or ſore bruiſed on their Shoulders, either by going on the hard Ground, by a cruſh of a Poſt or Gate, let them but bleed on the Fore-legs, it ſhall certainly heal them.

CHAP. IV.

For a Beaſt that has accidentally gotten Venom either in his Tongue or Body.

YOur Ox will commonly gape, and eat no meat, but ſtand holding his head and mourn, if he has eat any venemous Graſs or ſuch like, for Cure whereof give him to ſwallow down a white Onion bruiſed, well mixt with a little good Vinegar, but be ſure before he has it, you rub his Mouth and Tongue well with it.

BY taking Cold after a great Rain, by some Sicknefs or Surfeit, your Oxen, Kine or other Cattel may be loufie; for a Remedy, rub and chafe the Beaft all over with the Decoction of wild Olives mixt with Salt, or take Penniroyal mixt with Garlick ftampt. Give it the Beaft in Ale or Beer, and chafe him a while after. Some fay Rain will kill them, if you lift Afhes on their Backs. If you feed your Cattel well, and put them into good pafture, it will not be long ere they are well. If they have Lice or Ticks about them, thefe Medicines above are very good to kill them with.

C H A P. VI.

Againft the Swelling of Cattel by eating of green Corn.

YOur Cattel will be in danger of Death (without fpeedy Remedy) if through negligence of the Keeper, they eat of Barley, Rie or Wheat, that is near ripe; for it will lie and fpout in their Maws, and caufe in them a mighty Swelling. To help them, fome drive them up and down, till they fee them affwage thereof and fo they recover. Some throw a new-laid Egg, fhell and all into the Beafts Mouth, and break it in his Mouth, making him fwallow it with Ale. Some give him a handful of Nettle-tops well beat, and ftrained with Wine or honied Water. Some Stamp or ftrain Juniper Leaves or green Berries with Wine, and give it the Beaft. Others give the Beaft in Ale or Beer, Soot and the hard Rone of a red Herring well beaten. All which are approved Remedies.

C H A P. VII.

For an Ox or other Beaft that have loft their Quide.

AN Ox or other Beaft will mourn, and eat nothing (becaufe he cannot digeft what he has already eaten) if he happen to lofe his Quide, as perhaps by fome occafion it may fall out of his Mouth. To remedy this, fome take part of the Quide out of another Beafts Mouth of the like nature; if it be a Cow wants her Quide, they
take

Detail of the Bradford Table Carpet. Made in England in the late sixteenth century, it was embroidered with silks on linen canvas.

His fleece of wool doth cloath us all,
Which keeps us all from extream cold;
His flesh doth feed both young and old:
His tallow makes the candels white
To burne and serve us day and night,
His skinne dith pleasure divers waies,
To write, to weare at all assaies,
His guts thereof do make whelestrings,
They use his bones to other things,
His hornes some shepherds will not loose,
Because therewith they patch their shoes.

from *The First Book of Cattell*, 1591
Leonard Mascell

THE WORME IN THE SHEPES FOTE, AND HELPE THEREFORE

There be some shepe, that hath a worme in his foote, that maketh hym halte. Take that shepe, and loke betwene his clese, and there is a lyttell hole, as moche as a greatte pynnes heed, and therin groweth fyue or syxe blacke heares, lyke an inche long and more; take a sharpe poynted knyfe, and slytte the skynne a quarter of an inche long aboue the hole and as moche benethe, and put thy one hande in the holowe of the fote, vnder the hynder clese, and set thy thombe aboue almooste at the slytte, and thruste thy fyngers vnderneth forward, and with thy other hand take the blacke heares by the ende, or with they knyues poynte, and pull the heares a lyttell and a lyttell, and thruste after thy other hande, with thy fynger and thy thombe, and there wyll come oute a worme lyke a pece of fleshe, nygh as moche as a lyttell fynger. And whan it is out, put a lyttel tarre into the hole, and it wyll be shortely hole.

from *The Book of Husbandry*, 1534
Master Fitzherbert

OF THE ORDERING OF PONDS,
FOR THE NOURISHMENT OF FISH

There is nothing that killeth Fish or maketh them to prosper worse then putrified, and stinking water: neither is there any thing which corrupteth water sooner then Weeds, Sedge, and such filthinesse being suffered to grow therein: Therefore it shall be good once in three yeares for to cleanse your Ponds of all manner of Weeds and filth, which with a small Boat and a sharpe hooke you may easily do at the fall of the Leafe, for to cut them in Spring doeth increase them. Now if your ponds be much subject to mudde, as for the most part those in clay Countries are, then it shall be good once in seven yeares to draine them, and lade them, and this would be done at the beginning of the Spring; and such Fish as you are willing and meane to preserve, you shall put into smaller pits or stewes, and the other dispose at your pleasure: then causing the mudde to be troden with mens feet as you tread Morter, you shall see all the Eeles rise aloft, which when you have taken also, then with Shovels and trough Spades cast out all the mudde and filth (which is a singular compasse for Land) upon the Banke: then sodde the bottome of the Pond, and the sides with greene soddes, and fixe them hard into the earth with small stakes of Sallow, and these sides will nourish the Fish exceedingly.

This done, if your Pond have not any fresh Spring in it, then you shall lade the water backe againe into it, and then drawing your stewes, take out your store of Fish, and put them again into

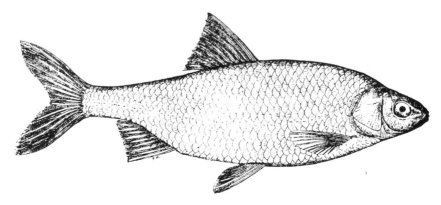

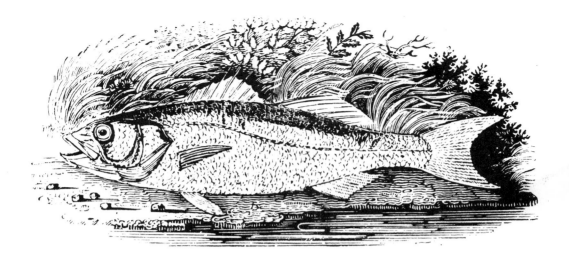

your Pond, observing ever that there be two parts spawners, and but a third melters.

These pits and small stewes, howsoever others write to the contrary, are better for feeding of Fish, then breeding: therefore you shall ever keep them with fresh water, and placing so one by another that you may empty them at pleasure, once in three monethes renew their bankes and bottomes with fresh sods of the fruitfullest grasse: also, you shall put into them good store of small Fry of Roch, Dace, Menowe, Loche, and Miller-thumbes: for the bigger Fish will feed thereon: also the inward Garbadge and blood of Sheepe, calves, Hogges, and such like, which will fat Fish suddainly, for you must know that as the Fish in Rivers have, by vertue of the current, ever something brought to them to feed on, so the Fish which is imprisoned in ponds and wants that helpe, must either be relieved, or else perish, and there is nothing better to feed them with, then that before spoken, or else Brewers graine, chippings, Curds, and any corne whatsoever, throwne into the Ponds morning and evening.

from *Country Contentments:*
or the Husbandmans Recreations, 1633
Gervase Markham

If Fish leap more than ordinary in Ponds or Rivers, it presageth Windes and Rain.

Prognosticks, 1669, **John Worlidge**

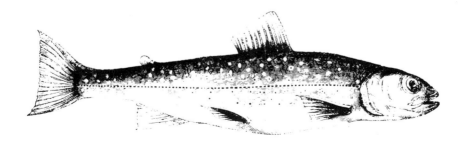

An illumination from a fifteenth century Belgian
treatise on agriculture.

THE HOUSE THAT JACK BUILT

This if the farmer sowing his corn,
That kept the cock that crowed in the morn,
That waked the priest all shaven and shorn,
That married the man all tattered and torn,
That kissed the maiden all forlorn,
That milked the cow with the crumpled horn,
That tossed the dog,
That worried the cat,
That killed the rat,
That ate the malt,
That lay in the house that Jack built.

Nursery rhyme

John Worlidge describes in 'Systema
Agriculturae', 1669, Gabriel Platt's invention for
drilling corn. He assures the reader that it would
be too hard for a woman or child to operate the
machine, but it would be useful if worked by one
man and one horse. This seed drill was produced
and used one hundred and fifty years before
Jethro Tull 'invented' the first commercial drill.

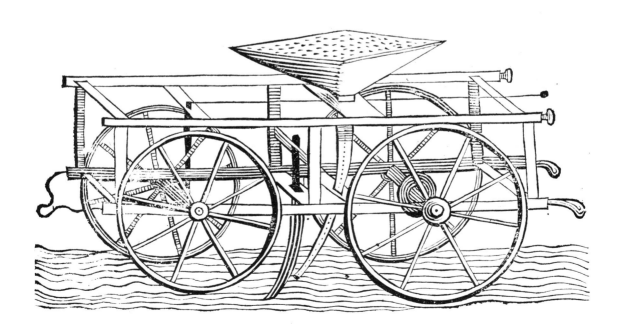

The Common Cart-Horse:
woodcut by **Thomas Bewick**

To inform these farmers that it is a very slovenly custom to let their pastures be over-run with bushes, mole and ant hills is surely needless: They must know that nothing would answer better than clearing away all rubbish of that sort; they know this, but have not the spirit, or at least the money to practice it. As to the hills and all little inequalities of the surface they should be pared off level, and nothing makes so fine a compost for all sorts of land as these turfs mixed with lime and dung; they should make a layer of them, about two foot deep, and length and breadth proportioned to the quantity, then bring a layer of lime eight inches deep over the turfs, then another layer of turfs two feet deep, then a layer of yard dung 18 inches deep, then another layer of lime eight inches deep; then a layer of turfs two feet deep; next a layer of York manure, cinder ashes, or mortar rubbish, 12 inches deep, and lastly, another of lime eight inches. This hill would be 12 feet high in the middle, as each layer should be made with a slope, particularly the first, for the rest to be right, that the carts might drive up easily; it should lay in this manner about two months, then it should be turned over and mixed; but on no account in the common way of doing that business. Let the men begin at one end, (or if there be a great number of them, along one side) and turn over the compost, cutting evenly thro' the layers, chopping to small pieces all the ant hills and turfs, mixing the pieces well with lime and dung, and when mixed, they must throw it from them parallel with the hill to have a clear space, a yard broad between the part mixed, and that to mix; when this beginning is made, some of the men should get on to the hill, and others remain in the vacant space, the former to throw down the compost, and the latter to chop and mix it, and then to give it a casting throw, like corn, on to the new made heap, that is finished. By these means all the kinds of manure will be thoroughly reduced to little pieces, and perfectly mixed together: If the work is well done, the compost will do without further mixing; though, as the expense of a second turning would be a trifle after it is so well reduced, and every turning would raise a fresh fermentation, a second would be adviseable: The farmer would be surprized at the vast benefit his crops would receive from a manuring of this compost after the draining; before that work is done it would be idle to do this or any other.

from *A Six Month Tour through Northern England*
Arthur Young (1741–1820)

If you see a white horse, spit three times for good luck.

If you see a piebald horse, spit over your right shoulder.

To step in horse dung means good luck.

Children's superstitions from
The Lore and Language of Schoolchildren, 1959
Iona and **Peter Opie**

Yet thou dost know
That the best compost for the lands
Is the wise master's feet and hands.

from *The Country Life*
Robert Herrick (1591–1674)

From the *Luttrell Psalter*, 14th century

Forty years ago, too, when a farmer came to buy a new farm, one of the things that he looked for on his first visit of inspection was the depth of muck in the yards. If it was less than a foot deep, he generally thought again before he bought the farm. At Peyton Hall, in Mr Waller's day, the muck was a good eighteen inches to two feet deep before it was carted. Yet the top layer was always sweet and clean straw for, every week throughout the year, except in the hottest days in summer, fresh straw was pitched into the yards, loads and loads of it, and roughly spread around so that there was no part where the old straw was still actually uncovered. The horses themselves were the best agents for spreading the straw for, when they were turned out of their stable after 'bait' in the evening, it was no uncommon sight to see all the twenty or two dozen of them rolling on their backs, flattening the straw out. In this way they rubbed freshness into their skins; but, as the week went on, and the straw became fouled by their defecations and urinations, you would notice that the horses did not roll so frequently as when the straw was first fresh. And all the time they were stamping their ordure and urine into the straw where it sank through to the bottom, rotting it all thoroughly, so that when the time of the muck-carting came, all the lower part of the once golden straw had assumed the rich colour and consistency of an old-fashioned plum pudding.

from *A Suffolk Childhood*, 1959
Simon Dewes

Lay compas up, handsomely, round on a hill,
to walk in thy yard, at thy pleasure and will;
More compas it maketh, and handsome the plot,
if horse-keeper, daily, forgetteth it not.

from *Five Hundred Good Points of Husbandry*, 1571
Thomas Tusser

Sunshine and shade: an illustration from *Chatterbox*, 1902

Beehive: woodcut by **Thomas Bewick**

'Nature's confectioner, the bee.'

from *Fuscara*
John Cleveland (1613–58)

Honey was the only form of sweetening
before sugar cane was produced commercially.
It was also an excellent base for a number
of very fine brews. Here is an extract from
Systema Agriculturae, *1669 by*
John Worlidge about the making of mead.

There are several ways of making curious Drinks or Liquors out of Honey, some make it white and cleer not onely by the pureness and finnees, and whiteness of the Honey, but also by some particular Process or Art they have, others make it very good, yet partly by reason of the nature and colour of the Honey, and partly for want of judgement, it carries with it a more gross and red tincture, but if the Honey be good, the tincture cannot be much injurious to the Drink.

Concerning the making whereof we have met with some few Directions, which we shall here insert.

A Receipt to make a pure Mead that shall taste like Wine.

Take one part of clarified Honey, and eight parts of pure Water, and boyl them well together in a copper Vessel, till half the Liquor is boyled away: but while it boyls you must take off the Scum very clean, and when it hath done boyling, and begins to cool, tun it up and it will work of itself, as soon as it hath done working you must stop the Vessel very close, and bury it under ground for three moneths, which will make it loose both the smell and taste of the Honey and Wax, and will make it taste very like Wine.

Another proportion.

Take of Honey clarified twenty pound, and of clear Water thirty two gallons, mingle them well together, and boyl that Liquor half away, and take off the Scum very clean, &c. and if you will have it of an Aromatick taste, you may add this proportion of ingredients, viz. Flowers of Elder, Rosemary, and Marjerom, of each an handful, of Cinamon two ounces, of Cloves six ounces, of Ginger, Pepper and Cardamon, each two scruples, these will give it a pleasant taste.

Courting Couple: woodcut by **Thomas Bewick**

Another proportion thus.

To a dozen gallons of the Scummed Must, take Ginger one ounce, Cinamon half an ounce, Cloves and Pepper of each alike two drams, all gross beaten, the one half of each being sowed in a bag, the other loose, and so let it boyl a quarter of an hour more.

    Some mix their Honey and Water till it will bear an egg, by which Rule you may make it stronger or smaller at pleasure.

THE PLOUGHMAN'S WOOING

Quoth John to Joan, wilt thou have me?
I Prithee now wilt, and Ise marry with thee:
My Cow, my Cow, my House and Rents,
And all my Lands and Tenements:
    Say my Joan, say my Joaney, will that not do?
    I cannot, cannot, come every day to woe.

I have Corn and Hay in the Barn hard by,
And three fat Hogs pend up in the sty;
I have a Mare and she's coal black:
I ride on her tail to save her back:

Say my Joan, say my Joaney, will that not do?
I cannot, cannot, come every day to woe.

I have a Cheese upon the shelf,
I cannot eat it all myself;
I have three good Marks that lie in a rag,
In the nook the Chimney instead of a bag:
    Say my Joan, say my Joaney, will that not do?
    I cannot, cannot, come every day to woe.

To marry I would have thy consent,
But faith I never could Complement;
I can say nought but hoy gee ho,
Terms that belong to Cart and Plough.
    Say my Joan, say my Joaney, will that not do?
    I cannot, cannot, come every day to woe.

Anon.

If Bees fly not far, but hover about home, it presageth Rain: or if they make more haste home than ordinary, a storm is at hand.

Prognosticks, 1669, **John Worlidge**

33

The Pigs in most esteem with farmers are those which will prove of a large size when fat; but I am convinced no sort is so profitable to a small family, or a poor man, as the Chinese, or a cross between that kind, and the breed of the country; because they are maintained and fatted on less food than others, and by a cross they will come to great size.

from *General View of the Agriculture of the County of Oxford*, 1794
Richard Davis

He gave it for his opinion, 'that whoever could make two ears of corn, or two blades of grass, to grow upon a spot of land where only one grew before would deserve better of mankind, and do more essential service to his country, than the whole race of politicians put together.'

from *Brobdingnag*
Jonathan Swift (1667-1745)

OF KEEPING A HEN FROM SITTING

If you would not have your Hen sit, you shall bathe her often in cold Water, and thrust a small Feather through her Nostrils.

from *The Country Gentleman's Companion*, 1753

     ... The careful hen
Calls all her chirping family around;
Fed and defended by the fearless cock,
Whose breast with ardour flames, as on her walks,
Graceful, and crows defiance. In the pond
The finely chequered duck before her train
Rows garrulous ...

     ... The turkey nigh,
Loud threat'ning, reddens; while the peacock spreads
His ever colour'd glory to the sun,
And swims in radiant majesty along.
Flies thick in am'rous chase, and wanton rolls
The glancing eye, and turns the changeful neck.

James Thomson (1700–48)

Now, shepherds, to your helpless charge be kind,
Baffle the raging year, and fill their pens
With food at will; lodge them below the storm,
And watch them strict; for, from the bellowing east,
In this dire season, oft the whirlwind's wing
Sweeps up the burden of whole wintery plains
At one wide waft, and o'er the hapless flocks,
Hid in the hollow of two neighbouring hills,
The billowy tempest whelms.

James Thomson (1700–48)

The Squeaking and skipping up and down of Mice and Rats, portend Rain.

Prognosticks, 1669, **John Worlidge**

At that time of day, all the single men lodged in the master's house, and were expected to conform to all the rules, regulations, hours, and work, of a well-regulated family.

Once in a year, the good farmer invited the married men, with their wives and families, to supper; and this supper was always the Harvest-Home. This was the day on which the last load of corn was conveyed into the barn or stack-yard, covered with green boughs, with shouting, and blowing of the merry harvest horn.

All the labourers upon the Priory Farm were assembled at six o'clock in the evening: nine married men, and five single ones; the wives, and those children who were old enough to come to the feast, together with the boys, four in number, who had to work upon the land.

A picture fit for the hand of Wilkie was exhibited in that ancient farm-house. It is surprising that no good artist should have painted the Harvest Supper. The Rent-day, Blindman's-buff, The Fair, The Blind Fiddler, or any of his celebrated works, he could scarcely afford a more striking subject for the canvass, or the printseller, than The Harvest Home. Such a scene may have been painted, but the writer of these pages had never seen it described, though he has often witnessed it in real life, and has shared with innocent pleasure in its rustic joy.

Margaret received great assistance from some of the married women. One pair of hands could not, indeed, have prepared sufficient eatables for such a party:- smoking puddings, plain and plum; piles of hot potatoes, cabbages, turnips, carrots, and every species of vegetable which the farmer's lands could produce – beef, roast and boiled, mutton, veal, and pork, everything good and substantial; a rich custard, and apple-pies, to which the children did ample justice, for all were seated round this well-furnished table in the old kitchen, celebrated for its curious roof and antique chimney-piece.

from *The History of Margaret Catchpole,*
a Suffolk Girl, 1846
Reverend Richard Cobbold

Any of us would kill a cow rather than not have beef.

Dr Samuel Johnson (1709–84)

The breezy call of incense-breathing Morn,
The swallow twittering from the straw-built shed,
The cock's shrill clarion, or the echoing horn,
No more shall rouse them from their lowly bed.

from *Elegy Written in a Country Churchyard*
Thomas Gray (1716–71)

If great numbers of the fry of Fish are generated in Lakes or Ditches where Fish rarely come, it presageth great scarcity of Corn, or death of Cattel.

Prognosticks, 1669, **John Worlidge**

THE AULD FARMER'S ADDRESS TO HIS
MARE MAGGIE

A Guid New Year I wish thee Maggie!
Hae, there's a rip to thy auld baggie:
Tho' thou's howe backit now, an knaggie.
   I've seen the day
Thou could hae gaen like ony staggie
   Out-owre the lay.

Robert Burns (1759-96)

TO A MOUSE

On turning her up in her nest with the plough,
November 1785

Wee, sleekit, cow'rin', tim'rous beastie,
O what a panic 's in they breastie!
Thou need na start awa sae hasty,
    Wi' bickering brattle!
I wad be laith to rin an' chase thee
    Wi' murd'ring pattle!

I'm truly sorry man's dominion
Has broken nature's social union,
An' justifies that ill opinion
    Which makes thee startle
At me, thy poor earth-born companion,
    An' fellow-mortal!

I doubt na, whiles, but thou may thieve;
What then? poor beastie, thou maun live!
A daimen-icker in a thrave
    'S a sma' request:
I'll get a blessin' wi' the lave,
    And never miss't!

Thy wee bit housie, too, in ruin!
Its silly wa's the win's are strewin':
And naething, now, to big a new ane,
    O' foggage green!
An' bleak December's winds ensuin'
    Baith snell an' keen!

Thou saw the fields laid bare and waste
An' weary winter comin' fast,
An' cozie here, beneath the blast,
    Thou thought to dwell,
Till, crash! the cruel coulter past
    Out thro' thy cell.

That wee bit heap o' leaves an' stibble
Has cost thee mony a weary nibble!
Now thou's turn'd out, for a' thy trouble,
    But house or hald,
To thole the winter's sleety dribble
    An' cranreuch cauld!

But, Mousie, thou art no thy lane
In proving foresight may be vain:
The best laid schemes o' mice an' men
    Gang aft a-gley,
An' lea'e us nought but grief an' pain,
    For promised joy.

Still thou art blest, compared wi' me!
The present only toucheth thee:
But, och! I backward cast my e'e
    On prospects drear!
An' forward, tho' I canna see,
    I guess an' fear!

Robert Burns (1759–96)

Great quantities of Frogs small or great,
appearing at unusual times, and in unusual
places, presage great Dearth of Corn, or
great Sicknesses to follow in that place
where they appear.

Prognosticks, 1669, **John Worlidge**

GRANFER GRIG

Granfer Grig
Had a pig
In a field of clover.
The pig he died,
Granfer cried,
And all the fun was over.

Cornish folk rhyme

THERE WAS A LADY LOVED A SWINE

There was a lady loved a swine.
Honey, said she,
Pig-hog, wilt thou be mine?
Hunc, said he.

I'll build for thee a silver sty,
Honey, said she,
And in it softly thou shalt lie.
Hunc, said he.

Pinned with a silver pin,
Honey, said she,
That you may go both out and in.
Hunc, said he.

When shall we two be wed,
Honey? said she.
Hunc, hunc, hunc, he said.
And away went he.

James Orchard Halliwell
The Nursery Rhymes of England, 1842
This song can be traced back to the early
seventeenth century.

An easy method of preventing pigs from rooting
is here practised by some gentlemen and
although a trifling circumstance, it may not be
thought unworthy of notice. The gristley or
horney part of the snout, through which the ring
is usually put, is cut away with a sharp knife; by
this means alone, without the least injury arising
from it to the animal, the mischief of rooting is
effectually prevented.

from *General View of the Agriculture of the
County Palatine of Chester*, 1794
Thomas Wedge

Of all the Creatures the Swine is most
troubled against Wind or Tempests, which
makes Countrey-men think that onely they
see the wind.

Prognosticks, 1669, **John Worlidge**

This little pig went to market;
This little pig stayed at home;
This little pig had roast beef;
This little pig had none;
And this tiny little pig went
Wee wee wee all the way home.

Nursery rhyme

Woodcut by **Thomas Bewick** (1752-1828)

Along the roads ...
Followed by dust like smoking clouds
Scotch droves of beast, a little breed
In sweltering weary mood proceed
A patient race from Scottish hills
To fatten by our pasture rills
Lean with the wants of mountain soil
But short and stout for travels' toil
Wi cocked up horns and curling crown
And dewlap besom hanging down
Follwed by slowly pacing swains
Wild to our rushy flats and plains
At whom the shepherds dog will rise
And shake himself, and in surprise
Draw back, and waffle in Affright
Barking the traveller out of sight
And mowers ore their scythes will bear
Upon their uncooth dress to stare
And shepherds as they trample bye
Leaves ore their crooks a wondering eye
In petticotes of banded plad
Wi blankets ore their shoulders slung
To camp at night the fields among ...

John Clare (1793–1864)

When the cuckoo comes to the bare thorn,
Sell your cow and buy your corn;
But when she comes to the full bit,
Sell your corn and buy your sheep.

North country saying

The mountain sheep are sweeter,
  But the valley sheep are fatter;
We therefore deemed it meeter
  To carry off the latter.

from *The Misfortunes of Elphin*
T. L. Peacock (1785–1866)

Sheep woodcut: **school of Thomas Bewick**

LAMBS AT PLAY

On the grassy banks
Lambkins at their pranks;
Woolly sisters, woolly brothers
Jumping off their feet
While their woolly mothers
Watch by them and bleat.

Christina Rossetti (1830–94)

THE LAMB

Little Lamb, who made thee?
Dost thou know who made thee?
Gave thee life, and bid thee feed
By the stream and o'er the mead;
Gave thee clothing of delight,
Softest clothing, wooly, bright;
Gave thee such a tender voice,
Making all the vales rejoice?
Little Lamb, who made thee?
Dost thou know who made thee?

Little Lamb, I'll tell thee,
Little lamb, I'll tell thee:
He is called by thy name,
For he calls himself a Lamb.
He is meek, and he is mild;
He became a little child.
I, a child, and thou a lamb,
We are called by his name.
Little Lamb, God bless thee!
Little Lamb, God bless thee!

William Blake (1757–1827)

If Land-fowl gather towards the Water,
and shake their Wings, making noises, and
washing themselves, it portendeth Tempests
at hand.

Prognosticks, 1669, **John Worlidge**

The poultry-yard – Duncan, 1847

They were the less restful cows that were stalled. Those that would stand still of their own will were milked in the middle of the yard, where many of such better behaved ones stood waiting now – all prime milchers, such as were seldom seen out of this valley, and not always within it; nourished by the succulent feed which the water-meads supplied at this prime season of the year. Those of them that were spotted with white reflected the sunshine in dazzling brilliancy, and the polished brass knobs on their horns glittered with something of military display. Their large-veined udders hung ponderous as sandbags, the teats sticking out like the legs of a gipsy's crock; and as each animal lingered for her turn to arrive the milk oozed forth and fell in drops to the ground.

from *Tess of the d'Urbervilles*
Thomas Hardy (1840–1928)

Richard Watson (1833–91), known as the bard of Barnard Castle, County Durham, at the height of his fame drew crowds of over ten thousand to hear him recite his poetry.

A COW HUNT

We've heard of many a gallant chase,
    Which in this neighbourhood took place;
But listen, and I'll tell you how
    Some Woodland colliers hunted a cow.

A merchant, Lowther was his name,
    To buy a cow to Pikestone came.
He bought it, as I've heard them say,
    The straightway homeward took his way.

When by Cust Burn and Foulsyke Pit,
    The cow took an unruly fit,
And turned to gore its master tried,
    But Lowther nimbly jumped aside.

O'er hedges, ditches, dykes and all,
    It bounced like an elastic ball,
And Lowther ran in hot pursuit
    In vain to turn the furious brute.

'Twas vain, for to Black Ling Hole it went,
    Its owner running till nearly spent,
And thus in an exhausted case,
    He compelled was to stop the chase.

He back to Woodland took his way,
    'Ten shillings,' he said, ' I'll freely pay,
To any party who will go,
    And bring her safe to Brumley Row.'

Four valiant colliers then set out,
    Of success they had not a doubt,
They searched the Bedburn Valley round,
    And in the woods the cow was found.

The cow, determined as before,
    With looks of contempt viewed them o'er,
She gave a bellow and made a bound,
    And knocked poor Priestley to the ground.

One Stephenson, with a pick-shaft armed,
    At matters soon became alarmed,
The crazy beast he durst not face,
    But ran off at his quickest pace.

One 'Joey' who was standing near,
    Retreated and gave way to fear,
'I mean not to be killed,' said he,
    And straightway he climbed up a tree.

When of his safety satisfied,
    'Cush-hope, cush-hope, cush-hope,' he cried.
Fixed on a bough like a baboon,
    He durst not for his life come down.

The other two, as it is said,
    Attached a halter to its head,
But the fierce brute on freedom bent,
    Soon slipped the rope and off it went.

Thus baffled quite, what could they do,
    But leave the victory with the cow?
Resolving as they left the place,
    Next morning to resume the chase.

But Captain Danby and his band,
    Had a fresh expedition planned,
Along with Dowson and Joe Gill,
    Two persevering men of skill.

Although 'twas rather dark and late,
  For morning they chose not to wait;
And Danby his own cow drove on
  To where they found the hunted one.

In company the cross beast soon
  Began to graze and settle down
Which did the wily hunters please,
  And they drove home the two with ease.

Next morning at the break of day,
  Nigh thirty colliers took their way,
With sticks well armed, a motley crew,
  The poor, dumb creature to subdue.

One Simpson was in such great haste,
  His breakfast he'd not time to taste,
A box hat he put on his head,
  And for the scene of action sped.

His hair was thin, therefore his hat
  Uneasy on his cranium sat.
It fell off and at this mishap
  He threw it down and borrowed a cap.

By Pennington and Black Ling Hole,
  Neath shaggy oaks and larches tall,
They vainly wandered up and down,
  And thus they spent the whole forenoon.

But when they came to understand
  How they'd been tricked by Danby's band,
They cursed and swore and left the place,
  Thus ended this most famous race.

From this a lesson we must draw,
  This strange cow hunt will plainly show,
When brute force will not stand the test,
  You'll find that gentle means are best.

'WHERE ARE YOU GOING, MY PRETTY MAID?'

'Where are you going, my pretty maid?'
'I'm going a milking, Sir', she said.
'May I go with you, my pretty maid?'
'You're kindly welcome, Sir', she said.
'What is your father, my pretty maid?'
'My father's a farmer, Sir', she said.
'What is your fortune, my pretty maid?'
'My face is my fortune, Sir', she said.
'Then I cannot marry you, my pretty maid'
'Nobody asked you, Sir', she said.

Anon.

Early nineteenth century etching of a milk vendor
from Middlesex.

Four ducks on a pond,
A grass-bank beyond,
A blue sky of spring,
White clouds on the wing:
What a little thing
To remember for years –
To remember with tears!

from *A Memory*
William Allingham (1828–89)

A MOTHERLESS SOFT LAMBKIN

A motherless soft lambkin
Alone upon a hill;
No mother's fleece to shelter him
And wrap him from the cold:–
I'll run to him and comfort him,
I'll fetch him, that I will;
I'll care for him and feed him
Until he's strong and bold.

Christina Rossetti (1830–94)

THE COW

The friendly cow, all red and white,
I love with all my heart:
She gives me cream with all her might,
To eat with apple-tart.

Robert Louis Stevenson (1850–94)

Goosey goosey gander,
Whither shall I wander?
Upstairs and downstairs,
And in my lady's chamber.
There I met an old man
Who would not say his prayers;
I took him by the left leg,
And threw him down the stairs.

Nursery rhyme

A ploughing match on Mr White's farm in Mickleover, Derbyshire, 1843. These competitions were very popular during the nineteenth century.

Men do not like hard work, but every man has an exceptional respect for tillage and a feeling that this is the original calling of his race.

from *Farming*
Ralph Waldo Emerson (1803–82)

Husbandry has in our time been glorified in eloquence which for the most part is vain, endeavouring as it does, to prove a falsity – that the agricultural life is, in itself favourable to gentle emotions, to sweet thoughtfulness, and to all the human virtues. Agriculture is one of the most exhausting forms of toil, and in itself, by no means conducive to spiritual development.

from *The Private Papers of Henry Ryecroft*
George Gissing (1857–1903)

THE PLOUGH
A LANDSCAPE IN BERKSHIRE

Above yon sombre swell of land
  Thou see'st the dawn's grave orange hue,
With one pale streak like yellow sand,
  And over that a vein of blue.

The air is cold above the woods;
  All silent is the earth and sky,
Except with his own lonely moods
  The blackbird holds a colloquy.

Over the broad hill creeps a beam,
  Like hope that gilds a good man's brow;
And now ascends the nostril-stream
  Of stalwart horses come to plough.

Ye rigid Ploughmen, bear in mind
  Your labour is for future hours:
Advance – spare not – nor look behind –
  Plough deep and straight with all your powers!

Richard Henry Horne (1803–84)

Of all things from which gain is obtained, nothing is better than agriculture, nothing more productive, more delightful, more worthy of a man or a freeman.

from *De Officiis*
Marcus Tullius Cicero (106–43 BC)

Oxen are so little used as scarce to make an exception. Mr Bower, of West Drayton, however cultivates a forest farm of 100 acres entirely with four oxen, and is very well satisfied with them; they work wholly on straw and grass, and do an acre a day in winter, and five roods in the spring. They are used two in the morning, and two in the afternoon.

from *General View of the Agriculture of the County of Nottingham*, 1798
Robert Lowe

There is very great difficulty in obtaining the truth on this head: farmers, like other people in business, are shy in laying open their affairs to anyone, and now more so than ever: in the first place, for fear their landlords should get hold of it, and thus be the means of an advance in their rent the first opportunity; and, in the second place, for fear of the Commissioners of the Income Tax should be made acquainted with it, and raise the duty on them. Farmers in general keep no books in a minute or regular manner; it is not therefore in their power to give the particulars of their expense and profit correctly, only in a rough way.

from *General View of the Agriculture of the County of Warwick*, 1813
Adam Murray

The glory of the farmer is that in the division of labours it is his part to create.

from *Farming*
Ralph Waldo Emerson (1803–82)

Sheep of all animals in the world express two things: the natural subject of civilisation and culture, and the equality of acceptance, of bowing to necessity. Anyone who has killed as many sheep as I have will know this last quality well. Even when the knife is at its throat the sheep does not struggle: it makes no sound while its throat is being cut. It accepts death as no other animal on earth.

from *The Heart of the Hunter*, 1961
Laurens van der Post

What, then, is this 'an improvement', is a nation richer for the carrying away of the food from those who raise it, and giving it to bayonet men and others, who are assembled in great masses? I could broom-stick the fellow who would look me in the face and call this an 'improvement'. What! was it not better for the consumers of the food to live near to the places where it was grown?

from *Rural Rides*
William Cobbett (1763–1835)

In every way agriculture is the first calling of mankind; it is the most honest, the most useful, and consequently the noblest which he can exercise.

from *Emile*
Jean-Jacques Rousseau (1712–78)

A farmer, according to his definition,
is a man who makes money on the farm
and spends it in town.
An agriculturalist is a man
who makes his money in town
and spends it on a farm.

from *Toaster's Handbook*
compiled by Peggy Edmund
and Harold Workman Williams

Jonathan Whistler, great grandfather of Rex Whistler, was a builder and decorator and lived in Sherbourne in Dorset. In the 1840's he became interested in photography, and took what might well be a set of the earliest photographs of English farm labourers in existence. The photographs were long neglected and unfortunately their quality has suffered as a result.

W. H. Hopkins Haymaking 1882

I saw also at Coleshill, the most complete farm yard that I ever saw, and that I believe there is in all England, many and complete as English farmyards are. This was the contrivance of Mr Palmer, Lord Folkestone's bailiff and steward. The master gives all the credit of plantation, and farm to the servant; but the servant ascribes a good deal of it to the master. Between them, at any rate, here are some most admirable objects in rural affairs. And here, too, there is no misery amongst those who do the work; those without whom there could have been no Locust-plantations and no farm-yard. Here all are comfortable; gaunt hunger stares no man in the face. That same disposition which sent Lord Folkestone to visit John Knight in the dungeons at Reading, keeps pinching hunger away from Coleshill. It is a very pretty spot all taken together. It is chiefly grazing land; and, though the making of cheese and bacon is, I dare say, the most profitable part of the

farming here, Lord Folkestone fats oxen, and has a stall for it, which ought to be shown to foreigners, instead of the spinning jennies. A fat ox is a finer thing than a cheese, however good. There is a dairy here too, and beautifully kept. When this stall is full of oxen, and they are all fat, how it would make a French farmer stare! It would make even a Yankee think, that 'Old England' was a respectable 'mother' after all. If I had to show this village off to a Yankee, I would blindfold him all the way to, and after I got him out of, the village, lest he should see the scarecrows of paupers on the road.

from *Rural Rides*
William Cobbett (1763–1835)

Potato-planting, 1844

Howe shall ye knowe seasonable tyme? (to sowe)
Go uppon the lande, that is plowed and if it
synge or crye, or make any noyse under thy
fete, then it is too wete to sowe; And if it
makes no noyse and wyll beare thy horses,
thanne sowe in the name of God.

from *The Book of Husbandry*, 1534
Master Fitzherbert

If the brest bone of a Duck be red, it
signifies a long Winter, if white the contrary.

Prognosticks, 1669, **John Worlidge**

The wind, the rain, the sun,
Their genial task have done,
  Wouldst thou be fed,
Man, to thy labour bow,
Thrust in thy sickle now,
Reap where thou once didst plough,
  God sends thee bread.

Robert Montgomery (1807–55)

The opinion that anything British is automatically superior to anything foreign is dramatically underlined by these two mid nineteenth century illustrations of the scraggy continental and plump British pig.

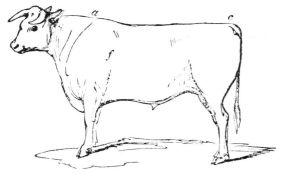

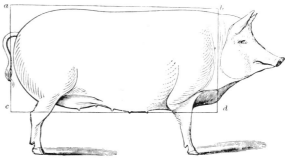

THE RECTANGLE TO ILLUSTRATE THE SYMMETRY OF THE PIG.

The end views of the best formed pigs are quite rectangular, though the generality of those met with in the country have the tendency to a larger rectangle in the fore than in the hind view. The view from above is also rectangular, except in the case of pigs having thick shoulders.

from *The Book of the Farm*, 1844
Henry Stephens

But assistance may be afforded you in ascertaining the weight of your cattle until you are better taught by experience, and this consists in measuring their bulk, or in weighing their live-weight. The live-weight of cattle is easily acertained by placing the animals upon a steel-yard, of which convenient forms have been recommended for the special purpose; but I am not aware that any of those which have been specially recommended are as accurate or convenient as might be. The rule to determine the quantity of beef by live-weight is to multiply the gross weight by .605 of a decimal, if the ox is ripe fat, but if not so, by .5 of a decimal; that is to say, that the offals of an ox in ordinary condition weigh about as much as its beef and bones. An ox should not be weighed immediately after it has fed, as it will weigh too heavy, but after it has chewed the cud, and is ready again to feed. Ascertaining the weight by measurement is a more convenient method than by weighing; and when the measurement is properly taken, and the ox of an ordinary size, it is about as accurate, though every person cannot measure an ox, that process requiring judgement to do it properly and accurately. Suppose the figure to represent an ox whose weight, sinking offals, is desired to be ascertained by measurement. The mode is, measure with a tape line from the top of the shoulder a to the tail-head c, and mark this for the length, then measure round the body at f, immediately behind the shoulder, and mark this for the girth, and on consulting the tables calculated for the purpose of affording the results, the weight of beef will be found. Upon what principle this rule for measurement is founded I cannot say, and suspect that it is entirely empirical. The rules by which the tables are calculated seem to be these two, namely; – multiply the square of the girth in inches by the length in inches, and divide the product by 7344, and the quotient is the weight in imperial stones. Or, square the girth in feet and multiply again by the decimal .238, and the sum is the weight of beef in imperial stones. For example: suppose the girth is 7 feet, or 84 inches, and the length 5 feet, or 60 inches, the weight of beef in imperial stones, according to Strachan's tables, which are the most recent, is 57 st. 10 lb. by the former rule, and by the latter it is 56 st. 4 lb. These results shew that there is no fixed principle upon which either rule is founded.

from *The Book of the Farm*, 1844
Henry Stephens

The Irish Cow Doctor –
drawn by **E. Fitzpatrick,** 1857

POOR BEASTS!

The horse and the mule live thirty years
And nothing know of wines and beers.
The goat and sheep at twenty die
And never taste of Scotch or Rye.
The cow drinks water by the ton
And at eighteen is mostly done.
The dog at fifteen cashes in
Without the aid of rum and gin.
The cat in milk and water soaks
And then in twelve short years it croaks.
The modest, sober, bone-dry hen
Lays eggs for nogs, then dies at ten.
All animals are strictly dry:
They sinless live and swiftly die;
But sinful, ginful, rum-soaked men
Survive for three score years and ten.
And some of them, a very few,
Stay pickled till they're ninety two.

Anon.

Cures like a charm Colic or Gripes, Shivering
Fits, and Chills in Horses and Cattle; instantly
relieves Hoven or Blown Cattle and Sheep; stops
Scour in, and is the best general Stimulant and
Tonic for, Calves and Lambs.

Matchless as a Restorative and Painkiller after
Lambing and Calving; for Fatigue in Hunters
and overworked Horses and in all cases where
Nature flags.

Taken from an advertisement for Days' Black Drink,
about 1880.

*In the eighteenth and nineteenth centuries,
blood letting with the aid of leeches was regularly
prescribed by physicians of the day for a great
many ailments. The young ladies in the
illustration are farm girls hunting for leeches
using their feet and legs as bait. When caught,
the leeches were put into the barrels of water
carried by each girl and sold at a good price to
the medical profession.*

Vaccinating a sheep, nineteenth century.

Olive and her stepdaughter Florence of Bildeston, Suffolk

Suffolk sheep near Stowmarket.

SHEEP AND LAMBS

All in the April evening,
April airs were abroad;
The sheep with their little lambs
Pass'd me by on the road.

The sheep with their little lambs
Pass'd me by on the road;
All in an April evening
I thought on the Lamb of God.

The lambs were weary, and crying
With a weak human cry,
I thought on the Lamb of God
Going meekly to die.

Up in the blue, blue mountains
Dewy pastures are sweet:
Rest for the little bodies,
Rest for the little feet.

But for the Lamb of God
Up on the hill-top green,
Only a cross of shame
Two stark crosses between.

All in the April evening,
April airs were abroad;
I saw the sheep with their lambs,
And thought on the Lamb of God.

Katherine Tynan Hinkson (1861–1931)

During the hard history of British farming, one of the most catastrophic periods must have been the great Irish potato crop failures of 1845, 1846 and 1849 when it was estimated that over a million farm workers and farm tenants died of starvation or malnutrition.

By the nineteenth century, the Irish people had become so dependent on the potato that when the potato crop first failed in 1845, 80% of the Irish agricultural output disappeared. Most of the small farmers were tenants, and consequently were unable to pay their rents.

A distant government in Westminster led by a cold Prime Minister, Robert Peel, and advised by the permanent head of the treasury, Charles Edward Trevelyan, sought to save the English tax payer and make the Irish fund their own calamity. They insisted that relief funds should come from an increased levy on the Irish rates. As the Irish rate payers were the land owners, they demanded their rents from tenants who, owing to the crop failure, were unable to pay. This forced many normally reasonable landlords to evict their tenants to raise more profitable crops in order to pay the rates.

It must of course be said that there were many unscrupulous absentee landlords in England who saw the eviction of their unprofitable tenants over the sea in Ireland as an easy way to clear their lands to make money. The result was that thousands of poor tenant farmers were evicted from their homes with nothing and left to starve in the streets. Within three years of the outbreak of the famine, it has been estimated that the population of Ireland dwindled by between two and three million people. At least a million died in the famine, and approximately one and a half million emigrated to the New World. The events of those three years probably did more to sour relations between the Irish and English people than any other event in Anglo-Irish history.

Justice to Ireland
'She gave them some broth without any bread,
Then whipp'd them all round, and sent them to bed.'

April 18th, 1846: *Punch*

top left: a typical scene of an Irish farmyard and farmhouse in the mid nineteenth century.
bottom left: an old lady sitting in the midst of her deserted village after eviction, Ireland, mid nineteenth century.

top right: an Irish farmhouse being battered to the ground after the tenants had been evicted. This was a common practice to stop the displaced tenants returning to their home for shelter.
bottom right: an evicted family in Ireland in the mid nineteenth century living in a peat hovel.

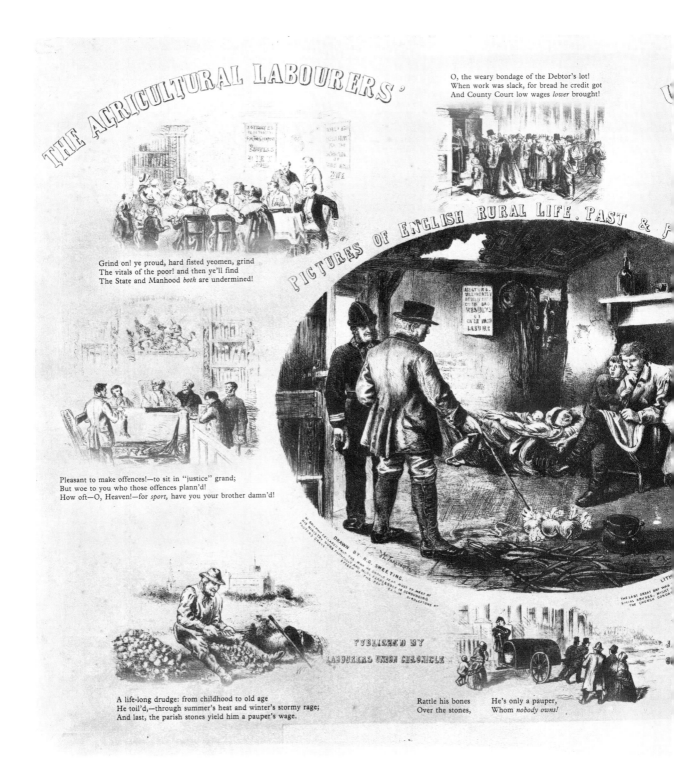

THE AGRICULTURAL LABOURERS'

PICTURES OF ENGLISH RURAL LIFE, PAST &

O, the weary bondage of the Debtor's lot!
When work was slack, for bread he credit got
And County Court low wages *lower* brought!

Grind on! ye proud, hard fisted yeomen, grind
The vitals of the poor! and then ye'll find
The State and Manhood *both* are undermined!

Pleasant to make offences!—to sit in "justice" grand;
But woe to you who those offences plann'd!
How oft—O, Heaven!—for *sport*, have you your brother damn'd!

DRAWN BY R.G. SWEETING.

PUBLISHED BY
LABOURERS UNION CHRONICLE

A life-long drudge: from childhood to old age
He toil'd,—through summer's heat and winter's stormy rage;
And last, the parish stones yield him a pauper's wage.

Rattle his bones
Over the stones,

He's only a pauper,
Whom *nobody owns!*

66

MOVEMENT – 1872

A Heaven-born Hope is sent!—*The world is wide!*
Awake they manhood's might! In manly pride
Go forth! and GOD will be thy Guide.

In vain Repression damps the stubborn soul!
Man's inhumanities, man yields back the whole
And crushing heart and mind, is made a *ghoul!*

And if his wearied patience break in discontent,
Suspicion haunts him—not encouragement:
And Hope all gone—to *Drink* the wretch is sent.

CASES HEARD AT ONE SITTING OF A
COUNTY MAGISTRATES' BENCH IN 1873.

George Major, agricultural labourer, fined 6s. and 9s. costs for unlawfully leaving his work. Defendant said he could not live on his wages. Defendant's wife (a delicate-looking young woman, with an infant in her arms) described their cottage as being in a miserable state, and she had caught her death through it. They had to hang up three old guano bags for protection from the weather. – Henry Ballard was fined 6d. and 5s. 6d. costs for trespassing in pursuit of game. Defendant said he hoped the Bench would be merciful, as he had but 11s. a-week to support 13 children, besides himself and wife. His wife was in a consumption, and she very much wished for a rabbit. The 'merciful' Bench allowed a fortnight for payment. – Elizabeth Vokins was sent to prison for 14 days for a stealing some pieces of brass belonging to a threshing machine. Defendant's husband said his wages were 11s. per week, and he had 6 children.

from a report on Newbury Petty Sessions, Berkshire, in the *Labourers' Union Chronicle*, March 15th, 1873.

THE RIVALS
PRIZE PEASANT versus PRIZE PIG

We are afraid that a similar rivalry obtains
even to this day at most of our Agricultural shows.

PUNCH 1847

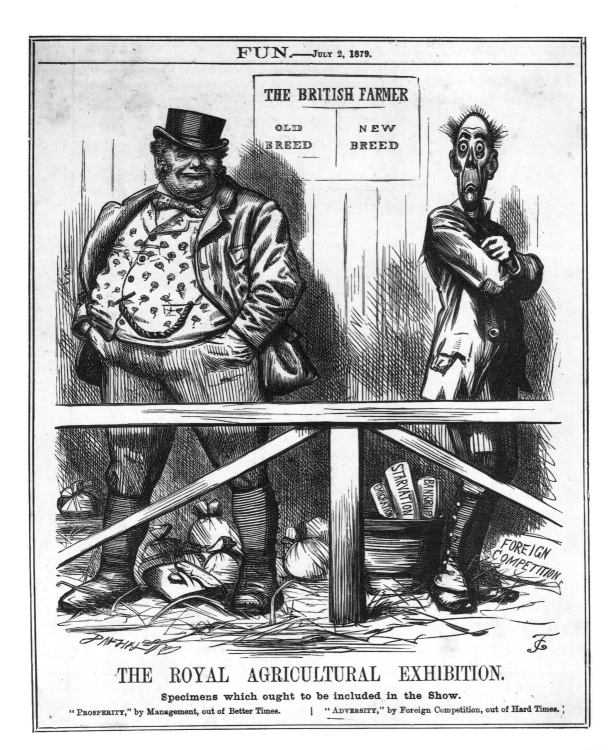

THE BRITISH FARMER

OLD BREED

NEW BREED

STARVATION

EMIGRATION

BANKRUP[?]

FOREIGN COMPETITION

THE ROYAL AGRICULTURAL EXHIBITION.

Specimens which ought to be included in the Show.

"PROSPERITY," by Management, out of Better Times. | "ADVERSITY," by Foreign Competition, out of Hard Times.

The Pig and the Peasant
Peasant: 'Ah! I'd like to be cared vor half as
well as thee be.'

LOCK-OUT AND AGRICULTURAL STRIFE

Although the protective Corn Laws had been repealed thirty years before, it was not until the late 1860's that, with improving sea and rail transport, the effect of cheap imported food from America and elsewhere was experienced by the British farming community. From the late 1860's the competition became so severe that the British farmers were forced to reduce their prices drastically, and as always the farm labourers suffered.

In 1872, in the village of Exning, in Suffolk, a letter was sent by 17 labourers to the farmers of Exning. It read as follows:

'Sir, –

'We, the undersigned, do hereby jointly and severally agree to call your attention to the following requirements for our labour – namely, 14s. for a week's work, and no longer to conform with the system of breakfasting before going to work during the winter quarter.

'Hoping you will give this your consideration and meet our moderate requirements amicably,

'Your humble servants – '

This so infuriated the local farmers that they immediately formed a Farmers' Association and refused to have anything to do with the labourers. The labourers were unable to live on their 12 shillings a week, and many of them watched as their families starved to death. The situation deteriorated, and in April 1873 the now Association of Essex and Suffolk Farmers stated:

'That the members of the Association pledge themselves not to pay more than 2s. a day of twelve hours, including breakfast and dinner for day work. That in the opinion of this meeting the members of the Association should resist the interference of the National Labourers' Union by discharging the men in their employ belonging to the said Union, after giving them a week's notice of withdrawal.'

At first some workers renounced their union and went back to work. Seeing their undernourished families fade before their very eyes, on March 19th 1874 the men of Exning insisted once again on at least one more shilling a week. The farmers refused and locked them out. All over East Anglia other farm labourers requested the same modest increase; again and again the farmers locked them out. The lock-out covered an area from the Newmarket district to Essex, Suffolk, Norfolk, Lincolnshire, Bedfordshire, Oxfordshire, Hampshire, Dorset, Warwickshire and Gloucestershire, and it has been estimated that at least 10,000 labourers were thrown out of work and refused permission to return unless they agreed to work for the old fee and to renounce their union. There was great sympathy for the farm workers from the Church, Parliament and the general public, but little action. Eventually many of the men did return, but thousands left the land; many emigrated to Canada, and many more moved to the cities. British agriculture suffered because of this, and it only really overcame the effects of the great lock-out when the nation realised the importance of a home agricultural industry with the outbreak of hostilities in 1914.

Before leaving the subject, it would be only fair to point out that the farmers were not all bad.

They also suffered desperately from the cheap imports from America, many farms went bankrupt, and for a number of years there were derelict farms and wasted areas that were uneconomic to work all over the country.

Letters quoted from *A History of the English Agricultural Labourer 1870–1920*, **F. E. Green,** 1920

Farmer Brooks farmed one of the biggest farms in Berkshire in the second half of the nineteenth century, and because of the economic conditions had to keep a very tight control on the expenses. This was not always appreciated by the local people. It was the custom for employers to brew the beer for the farm workers. Not surprisingly this was sometimes resented, particularly if the beer appeared rather weaker than the beer from the local inn. A local chant went:

Farmer Brooks of Bedlam Farm,
Brews his beer without any barm,
Feeds his cows on musty hay
And works his men without any pay.

His son seems to have been equally exacting – his instructions to a new worker on his first day were:

First, you milk the cows, then you
clean out and feed the pigs, then you
sweep the yard, after that, you
shepherd the sheep and feed the horses
– then you can go home to breakfast.

The above verses were related by Mr John Brooks of Oakham, Leicestershire, grandson of Farmer Brooks

The Agricultural Lock-Out – a Suffolk farmer and his men. A sketch near Bury St. Edmunds, 1874.

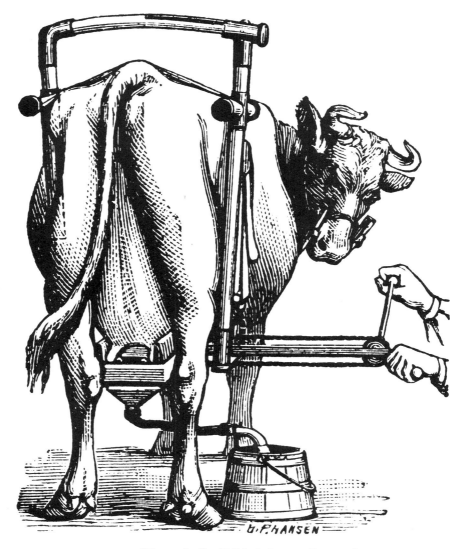

Danish Milking Machine

Animals are such agreeable friends – they ask no questions, they pass no criticisms.

from *Mr Gilfil's Love-Story*
George Eliot (1819–80)

A swine doth sooner than a cow
Bring an ox to the plough.

Medieval Gloucestershire saying

Preparing a bull for Smithfield Market

Ploughing with pigs in Belgium, c.1870

Hornsby's steam-powered thresher, 1851

Steam engines: during the middle of the nineteenth century, it was realised that steam could be used profitably to work the land. Steam engines proved so successful that some were still being used on farms in Britain until the outbreak of the Second World War.

74

Aveling's traction engine

Ransome and Sims' portable steam engine.

Welsh pigsty

P was a Pig, with a tail so curly;
Sometimes he was good,
    and sometimes surly.

Edward Lear (1812–88)

There was a Young Lady of Bute,
Who played on a silver-gilt flute;
She played several jigs
To her uncle's white pigs,
That amusing Young Lady of Bute.

Edward Lear (1812–88)

In the eighteenth and nineteenth centuries,
beekeeping became a fashionable pursuit amongst
the middle and upper classes. During this same
period there was a great vogue for oriental
architecture, and for this reason many of the
hives were fashioned in an oriental style.

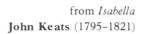

Even bees, the little almsmen of spring bowers,
Know there is richest juice in poison flowers.

from *Isabella*
John Keats (1795–1821)

The calf, the goose, the bee:
The world is ruled by these three.

Seventeenth century saying

How doth the little busy bee
Improve each shining hour,
And gather honey all the day
From every opening flower.

from *Against Idleness and Mischief*
Isaac Watts (1674–1748)

BEES

Every bee
that
ever was
was
partly
sting
and partly
... buzz.

from *Zoo Doings and Other Poems*
Jack Prelutsky, 1971

Drilling and Harrowing – Duncan, 1846

AS I WATCH'D THE PLOUGHMAN PLOUGHING

As I watch'd the ploughman ploughing,
Or the sower sowing in the fields, or the harvester harvesting,
I saw there too, O Life and Death, your analogies;
(Life, life is the tillage, and Death is the harvest according.)

Walt Whitman (1819–92)

A FARM PICTURE

Through the ample open door of the peaceful country barn,
A sunlit pasture field with cattle and horses feeding,
And haze and vista, and the far horizon fading away.

Walt Whitman (1819–92)

It was the new-fashioned agricultural implement called a horse-drill, till then unknown, in its modern shape, in this part of the country, where the venerable seed-lip was still used for sowing as in the days of Heptarchy. Its arrival created about as much sensation in the corn-market as as flying machine would create at Charing Cross. The farmers crowded round it, women drew near it, children crept under and into it. The machine was painted in bright hues of green, yellow, and red, and it resembled as a whole a compound of hornet, grasshopper, and shrimp, magnified enormously. Or it might have been likened to an upright musical instrument with the front gone. That was how it struck Lucetta. 'Why, it is a sort of agricultural piano,' she said.

from *The Mayor of Casterbridge*
Thomas Hardy (1840–1928)

When tillage begins, other arts follow. The farmers therefore are the founders of human civilisation.

Daniel Webster Remarks on Agriculture
January 13th 1840

I believe that a sensible peasant knows more about agriculture than authors who from the seculsion of their libraries issue instructions as to how the earth is to be ploughed.

Letters
Voltaire (1694–1778)

It used to be common practice to wash sheep before shearing. This was normally done in cold water and usually in a pool or stream. The picture shows late nineteenth century farmers preparing a ram for his 'dub', or wash, in a deep pool of a river in the Lake District.

JUNE 15TH

Today the sheep were dipped as a preventive of fly, for the bluebottle, to which most smells seem but as perfume, cannot bear the odour of the poisonous stuff wherein their fleeces are soaked. The process is rather curious: first the flock, as is usual on these great domestic occasions, are penned in the barn. Here two men seize the sheep one by one and plunge them legs upwards into a V-shaped tub half full of unpleasant-looking fluid. Now, indeed, the long-suffering sheep thinks that the end of all things is at hand. Its legs kick convulsively, its anxious ugly head projects from the yellow flood, while in the subdued light of the barn its eyes turn green with fright as it utters a succession of gurgling groans and baas. Next, it if be a ewe, so soon as the liquid has got a good bite of the skin she is lifted from the tub and set free, the roller on the edge of it preventing her from hurting herself however fiercely she may struggle. If, on the contrary, it is a lamb which has longer wool, it is laid upon the strainer, which, furnished with bars, is made of the cover of the bath and supported by a rest, where all superfluous fluid is squeezed from its fleece to run back into the tub. Then it is hoisted over the roller and departs into the field looking exactly as though it had developed a violent attack of jaundice.

from *A Farmer's Year*, 1899
Rider Haggard (1856–1925)

A nineteenth century Fell farmer with his lamb.

MY FATHER KEPT A HORSE

My father kept a horse and my mother kept a mare,
My brother kept a dog and my sister kept a hare,
Had a ride from the horse, a foal from the mare,
Pleasure with the dog and sport with the hare.

My father kept a bull and my mother kept a cow,
My brother kept a boar and my sister kept a sow,
Had beef from the bull and a calf from the cow,
Had bacon from the boar and pigs from the sow.

My father kept a buck, my mother kept a doe,
My brother kept a tup, my sister kept a ewe,
Had venison from the buck, fawn from the doe,
Had mutton from the tup, lamb from the ewe.

My father kept a cock, my mother kept a hen,
My brother kept a robin, my sister kept a wren,
Had chickens from the cock, eggs from the hen,
Had young ones from the robin, fed by the wren.

My father kept a cat, my mother kept a mouse,
My brother kept a flea, my sister kept a louse,
Had a scratch from the cat, had a squeak from the mouse,
Had a nip from the flea, had a bite from the louse.

                              Victorian ballad

*In medieval times, it was often the custom
to pull off the birds' feathers prematurely
to increase the feather yield. The feathers
grew again, but nevertheless it was a
distressing experience for the birds. This
practice was taken by Dutch settlers to the
New World, where it appears to have lasted
into the nineteenth century. This is
illustrated by the verse by Palmer Cox.*

One said, 'Those folk can hardly thrive,
Who pluck their poultry while alive.
For many a one, old dames have said
Has tossed through night a restless head,
The only sleepless one in town.
Because, on pillows made of down,
That cruel fingers had plucked loose
To music of the squawking goose.'

Palmer Cox (1840–1924)

The visiting knife sharpener at work,
Barnard Castle, late nineteenth century.

Shoeing a horse, near Barnard Castle,
County Durham, late nineteenth century.

The picture shows an elderly inhabitant flailing in Cumbria, late nineteenth century.

The Reeves fleecing machine, 1900.
There are still a few being used in isolated areas of the British Isles.

IN TIME OF 'THE BREAKING OF NATIONS'

Only a man harrowing clods
   In a slow silent walk
With an old horse that stumbles and nods
   Half asleep as they stalk.

Only thin smoke without flame
   From the heaps of couch-grass;
Yet this will go onward the same
   Though Dynasties pass.

Yonder a maid and her wight
   Come whispering by:
War's annals will cloud into night
   Ere their story die.

Thomas Hardy (1840–1928)

When the wind's in the west,
The weather's at the best;
When the wind's in the east,
It's neither gude for man nor beast;
When the wind's in the south,
Of rain there will be fouth;
When the wind's still,
No weather's ill.

Scottish proverb

THE SHEPHERD'S LAMENT

Full many a day I linger
On yonder mountain's brow,
Upon my crook all idly leaning,
And gaze in the valley below.

Then follow my flock as they're grazing,
My dog ever watches them well,
And find myself in the valley,
Yet how, I never can tell.

The meadow lies spread before me,
With lovely flow'rs of every hue;
I gather them, tho' without knowing
Whom I shall give them to.

And rain, and thunder, and lightning
I heed not under the tree,
But fondest hopes ever deceive me,
Yon door is ne'er open'd to me.

Bright arching above yon cottage
A rainbow gay doth stand,
But she has departed who dwelt there,
And far away over the land.

Far over the land or even,
Perhaps, far over the sea;
Go further, my sheep, pass by, pass by it;
Poor shepherd, ah; woe is me;
Go further, my sheep, pass by, pass by it;
Poor shepherd, ah, woe is me!

Goethe, translated by Dr Theodore Baker

Will Medhurst of Albourne, Sussex,
Champion Ploughman, 1938

On the day that I was eight years of age, I left school, and began to work fourteen hours a day in the fields, with from forty to fifty other children, of whom, even at that early age, I was the eldest. We were followed all day long by an old man carrying a long whip in his hand which he did not forget to use. A great many of the children were only five years of age. You will think that I am exaggerating, but I am not; it is as true as the Gospel. Thirty-five years ago (1850–60) is the time I speak of, and the place, Croyland in Lincolnshire, nine miles from

Peterborough. I could even now name several of the children who began at the age of five to work in the gangs, and also the name of the ganger.

We always left the town, summer and winter, the moment the old Abbey clock struck six. We had to walk a very long way to our work, never much less than two miles each way, and very often five miles each way. The large farms all lay a good distance from the town, and it was on those farms that we worked. In the winter, by the time we reached our work, it was light enough to begin, and of course we worked until it was dark and then had our long walk home. I never remember to have reached home sooner than six and more often seven, even in winter. In the summer we did not leave the fields until the clock had struck six, and then of course we must walk home, and this walk was no easy task for us children who had worked hard all day on the ploughed fields.

In all the four years I worked in the fields, I never worked one hour under cover of a barn, and only once did we have a meal in a house. And I shall never forget that one meal or the woman who gave us it. It was a most terrible day. The cold east wind (I suppose it was an east wind, for surely no wind ever blew colder), the sleet and snow which came every now and then in showers seemed almost to cut us to pieces. We were working upon a large farm that lay half-way between Croyland and Peterborough. Had the snow and sleet come continuously we should have been allowed to come home, but because it only came at intervals, of course we had to stay. I have been out in all sorts of weather but never remember a colder day. Well, the morning passed somehow. The ganger did his best for us by letting us have a run in our turns, but that did not help us very much because we were too numbed with the cold to be able to run much. Dinner-time came, and we were preparing to sit down under a hedge and eat our cold dinner and drink our cold tea, when we saw the shepherd's wife coming towards us, and she said to our ganger, 'Bring these children into my house and let them eat their dinner there.' We went into that very small two-roomed cottage, and when we got into the

largest room there was not standing room for us all, but this woman's heart was large, even if her house was small, and so she put her few chairs and table out into the garden, and then we all sat down in a ring upon the floor. She then placed in our midst a very large saucepan of hot boiled potatoes, and bade us help ourselves. Truly, although I have attended scores of grand parties and banquets since that time, not one of them has seemed half as good to me as that meal did. I well remember that woman. She was one of the plainest women I ever knew; in fact she was what the world would call quite ugly, and yet I can't think of her even now without thinking of that verse in one of our hymns where it says:

'No, Earth has angels though their forms are moulded
But of such clay as fashions all below,
Though harps are wanting, and bright pinions folded,
We know them by the love-light on their brow.'

Had I time I could write how our gang of children, one winter's night, had to wade for nearly half a mile through the flood. These floods occur nearly every winter, when the Wash overflows her banks. In harvest-time we left home at four o'clock in the morning, and stayed in the fields until it was dark, about nine o'clock. As a rule the gangs were disbanded during the harvest, each child going to work with its own friends, and when the corn was cut, the whole families would go gleaning the corn left in the fields, this being, of course, the gleaner's own property. A great many families gleaned sufficient to keep them in bread for the whole of the winter.

For four years, summer and winter, I worked in these gangs – no holidays of any sort, with the exception of very wet days and Sundays – and at the end of that time it felt like Heaven to me when I was taken to the town of Leeds, and put to work in the factory. Talk about White Slaves, the Fen districts at that time was the place to look for them.

from *Life as we have known it*, **Mrs Burrows**

Hay dragging: during the nineteenth century it
was not uncommon for the hay to be harvested
from the fields and dragged by pony or ox to the
farm. The distances were usually fairly short, but
the terrain very rough, and it was not worth the
risk of damaging a valuable vehicle in such a
hazardous operation.

The farm of Mr Neilson, of Halewood, exhibits several points worthy of notice. A light tramway with waggons is made use of for taking the turnip crop off the ground in moist weather. The tramway is readily shifted, and the crop is thrown into the waggons, which are then each pushed along by a man, so that the entire crop may be removed from the ground, which receives no injury from the feet of horses. The tramway can be constructed for 1s 4d per yard, and might be very advantageously introduced on all heavy farms where it is found difficult to take off the turnip crop in moist weather. A gang of men are at present employed on a considerable field of Mr Neilson's in taking off the turnip crop, which they draw from the ground, fill into the waggons, and convey outside of the gate at the rate of 6s an acre, shifting the tramway at their own cost. At this work they earn 2s 3d a day.

from *The Times*, 1850
Sir James Caird

Here stretched in ranks the swell'd swarths
  are found,
Sheaves heap'd on sheaves here thicken up
  the ground.
With sweeping stroke the mowers strew
  the lands;
The gatherers follow and collect in bands;
The rustic monarch of the field descries,
With silent glee, the heaps around him rise.

from a translation of the *Illiad* by
Alexander Pope (1688–1744)

It is generally thought to be lucky to meet a hay cart, but unlucky to see the back of the cart. This superstitious belief is expressed in rhyme form by the children of Pasadena, California:

Load of hay, load of hay,
Make a wish and turn away.

Casting down a stack, 1844

THE BLACK HEN

Hickety, pickety my black hen,
She lays eggs for gentlemen,
Gentlemen come every day
To see what my black hen doth lay.

Cock a doodle doo!
My dame has lost her shoe,
My master's lost his fiddling stick,
And knows not what to do.

HEN AND COCK

Hen: Cock, cock, I have la-a-a-yd.
Cock: Hen, hen, that's well sa-a-a-yd.
Hen: Altho' I have to go barefooted every da-a-y.
Cock: Sell your eggs, and buy shoes.
  Sell your eggs, and buy shoes.

Nursery rhymes

These Durham pipers are playing for alms outside the kitchen of a Barnard Castle house in the late nineteenth century. Wandering pipers were to be seen in Durham until the 1920s.

A gentleman of the road and gamekeeper, near Bildeston, Suffolk, late nineteenth century.

The cattle are grazing,
Their heads never raising,
There are forty feeding like one.

from *Written in March*
William Wordsworth (1770–1850)

It's by the mouth o' the cow that the milk comes.

Scottish proverb

Milking songs are peculiar to the Highlands of Scotland, and there appears to be an almost total absence of such songs in England and the Lowlands. Although occasionally in Lowland lyrics there is a mention of ewe milking, there is, curiously, no reference to the milking of cows. Milking songs are thought to have originated from the milkmaid's need to keep the cows calm while milking, and so the songs have soothing melodies, and are often flattering and complimentary to the cow. The following song comes from Ardnamurchan, on the west coast of Scotland.

Be nice, now, my cow,
Be nice, and be gentle,
Be quiet and gentle,
And all of you should be now –
 Of all pets the dearest!
She will get a nice wisp of hay,
And a soft bed of ferns from me,
With a drink of meal and crystal-clear water,
And meantime she will not refuse me her milk.

She will give me her milk,
Ay, her milk she will freely give me;
Fore leg fetter or hind feet shackles
Shall not be so much as mentioned
 in connection with my darling;
She will not lift a leg,
Nor will she show any ill-temper,
Such as is only shown by the nasty cows
That understand only the English language.

Soft and warm is the teat
Of my charming little cow;
Soft and warm, too, is her milk
Under its froth of delightfullest odour.
My dear and delight
Is the beautiful little heifer;
She has given me her promise
That she will not refuse me her milk.

Out to the grazing ground,
Out to the grazing ground,
Out to the grazing ground,
 To-morrow morning early!
The grass will reach well up to thy knee
In Doire-na-Giubhsaich,
She will thence carry home a full udder,
And sure I am that she will not thereof
 refuse me a fair, full share.

ICE HOUSES

Before gas and electricity were readily available, the ice house was the only way of preserving perishable food, particularly meat and dairy products. Ice house construction reached such a high standard that by the second half of the nineteenth century it was not uncommon for ice to keep for as long as ten months, and occasionally even a year. The principle was simple: as much ice as possible was packed around the ice room which was then well insulated. Sometimes the ice houses were built into the side of hills to assist in insulation. Usually ice was collected from frozen rivers and lakes in winter time, but subsequently ships used to load great slabs from the Arctic into their holds and rush them to the major ports of England and America, where they were transferred to trains and then carts on their rapid journey to their final destination.

SMOKING MEAT

This American idea for a small smoke house was simply an empty, bottomless wine barrel, fitted with two strong rods across the top inside. Over these rods rested between five and seven rails, and from these rails salted meat was hung. The bottomless barrel was placed half over a pit of smouldering oak saw-dust or chippings. The lid was placed over the top of the barrel, and the smoke was allowed to seep out from holes drilled in the top quarters of the barrel. If the heat became too intense, the barrel was eased sideways to reduce the opening to the embers. After some 36 hours, the ham and bacon were well-smoked. Care was taken not to allow the heat inside the barrel to exceed blood temperature, otherwise the meat would half cook and the fat would rapidly turn rancid.

Lakeland geese being driven to market, late nineteenth century. When geese and turkeys were
driven long distances on roads, their feet were
often dipped in tar as a protective measure.

THE OLD GRAY GOOSE

Go tell Aunt Nancy,
Go tell Aunt Nancy,
Go tell Aunt Nancy
Her old gray goose is dead.

The one she'd been saving,
The one she'd been saving,
The one she'd been saving
To make a feather-bed.

She died last Friday,
She died last Friday,
She died last Friday
Behind the old barn shed.

Old gander's weeping,
Old gander's weeping,
Old gander's weeping
Because his wife is dead.

She's left five little goslings,
She's left five little goslings,
She's left five little goslings
To scratch for their own bread.

Anon.

Milking men in Suffolk, late nineteenth century.

Now i will Show how the Labourers got their Pig. Then i will Show you How many men Fed them. The farmer would Let any many at the Latter end of Summer Have a small Pig ranging from twenty to thirty Shillings in value and let him pay it Back at sixpence a week. But to feed this pig the labourer took most of the Food from there Master. i Have se in one Labourer's House in 1846 a Sack of Beans, a Sack of Barley, a Sack of Wheat – all stolen from the master. Keeping these men in Poverty made them Thieves. Poverty is the Mother of invention. Poverty made me Poach.

from James Hawker's journal *A Victorian Poacher*

The rodent catcher and son, Suffolk, 1890.

Muck Carting: woodcut by **Thomas Bewick**

ID WISNA FUN

Spartan doung in days long gone –
'Efore mechanical spreaders took on –
Wis a balancing act 'at wisna fun,
   On a moovan kert;
But for 'e tatties id hed to be done,
   An' Beelag wis expert.

Ae day a faap wi' flappering wing,
Caused 'e gerran tae forward spring,
An' rearan up, 'e demented thing,
   Id couped 'e kert,
An' Beelag wi' his graipe aswing,
   Dived in 'e dirt.

Poor Beelag sure wis oot o' luck,
For lek a statue there he stuck,
Up till his oxters in 'e muck,
   An' swieran sair;
'E air aboot wis blue an' thick
   Wi' language rare.

'Etween wirsels id wis a sicht,
Seean owld Beelag in sic a plicht;
But lauchan aboot id widna be richt,
   Id wisna fun;
His troosers were left outside 'at nicht,
   But noor let on.

Geddes O'Mey, 1978

A plain country fellow is one that manures his ground well, but lets himself lie fallow and untilled. He has reason enough to do his business, and not enough to be idle or melancholy. He seems to have the judgement of Nebuchadnezzar: for his conversation is among beasts, and his talons none of the shortest, only he eats not grass, because he loves not sallets. His hand guides the plough, and the plough his thoughts, and his ditch and landmark is the very mound of his meditations. He expostulates with his oxen very understandingly, and he speaks Gee and Ree better than English. His mind is not much distracted with objects: but if a good fat cow come in his way, he stands dumb and astonisht, and though his haste be never so great, will fix here half an hour's contemplation.

from *Microcosmographie*, 1628, a collection of character sketches chiefly written by **John Earle** (1601?–65), bishop of Salisbury.

Money is like muck, not good except it be spread.

from *Of Seditions and Troubles*, **Francis Bacon** (1561-1626)

The men with the muck-rakes are often
indispensible to the well-being of society;
but only if they know when to stop raking
the muck.

> from a speech at the laying of a corner stone of
> the House of Representatives, 14th April 1906
> **Theodore Roosevelt** (1858–1919)

I have been in Egilsay, and I have been in Wyre,
But I've never been in Sanday where the coo dung's fire.

*A mainland jibe at the inhabitants of Sanday
(in the Northern Isles) where they used to
burn dried cow pats.*

Where there is muck there is luck.

> Old Scottish saying

And now the dairy claims her choicest care,
And half her household find employment there:
Slow rolls the churn, its load of clogging cream
At once forgoes it quality and name;
From knotty particles first floating wide,

Congealing butter's dash'd from side to side;
Streams of new milk through flowing coolers stray,
And snow-white curds abound, and wholesome whey.

from *The Farmer's Boy*,
Robert Bloomfield (1766–1823)

Suffolk ladies' butter making class, c. 1900.

THE GOOSE AND THE GANDER

O the goose and the gander walk'd over the green,
O the goose she went barefoot for fear of being seen,
For fear of being seen, boys, for fear of being seen,
And the goose she went barefoot for fear of being seen.

I had a black hen and she had a white foot,
And she laid an egg in a willow tree root,
In a willow tree root, in a willow tree root,
And she laid a white egg in a willow tree root.

from *Traditional Tunes*, **Kidson,** 1891

Grey goose and gander,
  Waft your wings together
And carry the good King's daughter
  Over the one-strand river.

Nursery rhyme

G is a little old Goose,
Who feeds all day upon grass;
And who makes no end of a hissing noise
At all the people who pass.

Edward Lear (1812–88)

The wild goose comes north with the voice
of freedom and adventure. He is more than
a big, far-ranging bird, he is the epitome of
wanderlust, limitless horizons and distant
travel.

Halborland

Ducks and Geese &c. picking their wings,
washing themselves much, or cackling much,
signifies Rain.

Prognosticks, 1669, **John Worlidge**

GOATS

I do not dote
Upon the goat
In fact I simply loathe him.
He has the most unpleasant tricks
The front end butts – the other kicks.
The very word caprine is fraught
With obviously obnoxious thought.
While ovine flocks are all that's nice
Goats are the embodiment of vice.

The Billy wears a wagging beard,
His bleating voice is quite absurd,
And when he reaches adult style
Emits effluvia simply vile.
I'm very glad I was not born
Beneath the sign of Capricorn
Because – I think
Goats STINK.

Phyllis Haynes, 1980

If the beard were all, the goat might preach.

Seventeenth century saying

113

One sometimes hears from persons of the chillier type of culture the remark that plain country people do not appreciate the beauty of the country. This is an error rooted in the intellectual pride of mediocrity; and is one of the many examples of a truth in the idea that extremes meet. Thus, to appreciate the virtues of the mob one must either be on a level with it (as I am) or be really high up, like the saints. It is roughly the same with aesthetics; slang and rude dialect can be relished by a really literary taste, but not by a merely bookish taste. And when these cultivated cranks say that rustics do not talk of Nature in an appreciative way, they really mean that they do not talk in a bookish way. They do not talk bookishly about clouds or stones, or pigs or slugs, or horses or anything you please. They talk piggishly about pigs; and sluggishly, I suppose, about slugs; and are refreshingly horsy about horses. They speak in a stony way of stones; they speak in a cloudy way of clouds; and this is surely the right way. And if by any chance a simple intelligent person from the country comes in contact with any aspect of Nature unfamiliar and arresting, such a person's comment is always worth remark. It is sometimes an epigram, and at worst it is never a quotation.

... A country girl I know in the county of Buckingham had never seen the sea in her life until the other day. When she was asked what she thought of it she said it was like cauliflowers. Now that is a piece of pure literature – vivid, entirely independent and original, and perfectly true. I had always been haunted with an analogous kinship which I could never locate; cabbages always remind me of the sea and the sea always reminds me of cabbages. It is partly, perhaps, the veined mingling of violet and green, as in the sea a purple that is almost dark red may mix with a green that is almost yellow, and still be the blue sea as a whole. But it is more the grand curves of the cabbage that curl over cavernously like waves, and it is partly again that dreamy repetition, as of a pattern, that made two great poets, Aeschylus and Shakespeare, use a word like 'multitudinous' of the ocean. But just where my fancy halted the

Buckinghamshire young woman rushed (so to speak) to my imaginative rescue. Cauliflowers are twenty times better than cabbages, for they show the wave breaking as well as curling, and the efflorescence of the branching foam, blind, bubbling and opaque. Moreover, the strong lines of life are suggested ... The first essential of the merely bookish view of the sea is that it is boundless, and gives a sentiment of infinity. Now it is quite certain, I think, that the cauliflower simile was partly created by exactly the opposite impression, the impression of boundary and barrier. The girl thought of it as a field of vegetables, even as a yard of vegetables. The girl was right. The ocean only suggests infinity when you cannot see it; a sea mist may seem endless, but not a sea. So far from being vague and vanishing, the sea is the one hard straight line of Nature. It is the one plain limit; the only thing that God has made that really looks like a wall.

from *A Shilling for My Thoughts*
G.K. Chesterton (1874-1936)

DUCKS' DITTY

Ducks' tails, drakes' tails,
Yellow feet a-quiver,
Yellow bills all out of sight
Busy in the river!

Kenneth Grahame (1859-1932)

PIPPA'S SONG

The year's at the spring,
And day's at the morn;
Morning's at seven;
The hill-side's dew-pearl'd;
The lark's on the wing;
The snail's on the thorn;
God's in His heaven –
All's right with the world!

Robert Browning (1812-89)

What price the bull? Suffolk, early 20th century

Prices in England since 1201 AD, by centuries

	13th	14th	15th	16th	17th	18th	19th
Ox	43s.	45s.	42s.	40s.	106s.	107s.	280s.
Cow	30s.	35s.	30s.	30s.	80s.	100s.	200s.
Horse	...	...	84s.	80s.	106s.	275s.	440s.
Sheep	3s.	4½s.	4s.	4s.	8s.	19s.	25s.
Pig	6s.	9s.	6s.	6s.	9s.	23s.	30s.
Wheat, quarter	...	16s.	12s.	21s.	45s.	53s.	56s.
Wine, gallon	3s.	3s.	2s.	4s.	6s.	17s.	20s.
Beer	3d.	5d.	4d.	4d.	4d.	8d.	18d.
Goose	9d.	12d.	12d.	11d.	12d.	25d.	50d.
Rabbit	6d.	6d.	6d.	4d.	6d.	8d.	12d.
Hen	3d.	6d.	6d.	5d.	9d.	12d.	18d.
Pigeons, dozen	9d.	12d.	12d.	12d.	13d.	18d.	36d.
Beef, 8 lbs.	6d.	12d.	10d.	8d.	25d.	38d.	64d.
Butter, lb.	...	4d.	3d.	3d.	4d.	5d.	12d.
Eggs, dozen	3d.	6d.	6d.	4d.	4d.	8d.	12d.

Note-Book of Agricultural Facts and Figures
for Farmers and Farm Students, 1910
Primrose McConnell

I went into the stable to see what I could see,
And there I saw three horses standing by one, two, and three.
I called unto my loving wife – I'm coming, sir, said she.
Pray, what do these three horses here without the leave of me?
Why, you old fool! blind fool! Can't you very well see?
They are three milking cows my granny sent to me.
 Ods bobs! What fun! Milking cows with saddles on!
  The like was never seen!
 If ever I go out from home a cuckold I come in.

I went into the kitchen to see what I could see,
And there I saw three hats hang by one, two, and three.
I called unto my loving wife – I'm coming, sir, said she.
Pray, what do these three hats here without the leave of me?
Why, you old fool! blind fool! Can't you very well see?
They are three milking pails my granny sent me.
 Ods bobs! What fun! Milking pails with brims on!
  The like was never seen!
 If ever I go out from home a cuckold I come in.

I went into the kitchen to see what I could see,
And there I saw three whips hang by one, two, and three.
I called unto my loving wife – I'm coming, sir, said she.
Pray, what do these three whips here without the leave of me?
Why, you old fool! blind fool! Can't you very well see?
They are three pokers my granny sent to me.
 Ods bobs! What fun! Pokers all with lashes on!
  The like was never seen!
 If ever I go out from home a cuckold I come in.

I went into the kitchen to see what I could see,
And there I saw three coats hang by one, two, and three.
I called unto my loving wife – I'm coming, sir, said she.
Pray, what do these three coats here without the leave of me?
Why, you old fool! blind fool! Can't you very well see?
They are three butter cloths my granny sent to me.
 Ods bobs! What fun! Butter cloths with buttons on!
  The like was never seen!
 If ever I go out from home a cuckold I come in.

I looked beneath the table to see what I could see,
And there I saw three pairs of boots by one, two, and three.
I called unto my loving wife – I'm coming, sir, said she.
Pray, what do these three pairs of boots without the leave of me?
Why, you old fool! blind fool! Can't you very well see?

They are three flower-pots my granny sent to me.
Ods bobs! What fun! Flower-pots with spurs on!
The like was never seen!
If ever I go out from home a cuckold I come in.

I went into the chamber to see what I could see,
And there I saw three strange men lie by one, two, and three.
I called unto my loving wife – I'm coming, sir, said she.
Pray, what do these three men here without the leave of me?
Why, old fool! blind fool! Can't you very well see?
They are three dairymaids my granny sent to me.
Ods bobs! What fun! Dairymaids with beards on!
The like was never seen!
If ever I go out from home a cuckold I come in.

Anon.

A Whitby farmer and milkmaid,
c. 1900;
Frank Meadow Sutcliffe

School children from Barnard Castle, County Durham, *c.* 1895

Little boy blue,
Come blow up your horn,
The sheep's in the meadow,
The cow's in the corn.
Where is the boy
Who looks after the sheep?
He's under a haycock
Fast asleep.

Little Bo-Peep has lost her sheep,
And doesn't know where to find them;
Leave them alone, and they'll come home,
Bringing their tails behind them.

Three blind mice, see how they run!
They all ran after the farmer's wife,
Who cut off their tails with a carving knife,
Did ever you see such a thing in your life,
As three blind mice?

A girl she would a hunting go,
With never a horse to ride;
She mounted on her father's boar,
And spurred him on the side.
Chink! chink! chink! the bridle went,
And chink! chink! chink! the little girl went
As she rode far and wide.

120

Hey diddle, diddle,
The cat and the fiddle,
The cow jumped over the moon;
The little dog laughed,
To see such sport,
And the dish ran away with the spoon.

I had a little hen, the prettiest ever seen,
She washed me the dishes and kept the
    house clean;
She went to the mill to fetch me some flour;
She brought it home in less than an hour;
She baked me my bread, she brewed me
    my ale;
She sat by the fire and told many a fine tale.

A donkey walks on four legs, and I walk on two,
The last one that I saw was just like you.
from *Nursery Rhymes of England* 1842

from *Nursery Rhymes of England* 1842
James Orchard Halliwell

Sweetly sings the donkey as he goes to grass,
He who sings so sweetly, is sure to be an ass.

from a nineteenth century autograph album

Gaffer Gilpin got a goose and gander.
Did Gaffer Gilpin get a goose and gander?
If Gaffer Gilpin got a goose and gander,
Where are the goose and gander
    that Gaffer Gilpin got?

Anon.

There was a Young Lady of Hull,
Who was chased by a virulent Bull;
But she seized on a spade,
And called out – "Who's afraid!"
Which distracted that virulent Bull.

Edward Lear (1812–88)

Tom, Tom, the piper's son,
Stole a pig and away he run;
The pig was eat, and Tom was beat,
And Tom went howling down the street

Anon.

There was an Old Man who said, "How –
Shall I flee from this horrible Cow?
I will sit on this stile,
And continue to smile,
Which may soften the heart of that Cow."

Edward Lear (1812–88)

THE FIVE HENS

There was an old man who liv'd in
    Middle Row,
He had five hens, and a name for them, oh!
Bill and Ned and Battock,
Cut-her-foot and Pattock.
Chuck, my lady Pattock,
Go to thy nest and lay.

from *The Nursery Rhymes of England*
James Orchard Halliwell

An when the children be too young to earn
A penny, they can g'out in sunny weather,
An' run about, an' get together
A bag o' cow-dung vor to burn.

William Barnes (1801–86)

D was a beautiful Duck
With spots all over his back;
He swam about in a beautiful pond,
And when he came out, said Quack.

Edward Lear (1812–88)

The mid Victorian English porkers, c. 1860

THE IRISH PIG

'Twas an evening in November,
As I very well remember,
I was strolling down the street in drunken pride,
But my knees were all a'flutter,
So I landed in the gutter,
And a pig came up and lay down by my side.

Yes, I lay there in the gutter
Thinking thoughts I could not utter,
When a colleen passing by did softly say,
'Ye can tell a man that boozes
By the company he chooses.' –
At that, the pig got up and walked away!

Anon, Dublin

JOHNNAG AN' HIS SOO

Did ee hear 'e latest farlie
    Aboot Johnnag an' his soo?
He geed an' lay doon 'eside her
    'E ither nicht fan he wis fu'.
Fan he laid his airm across her
    An' tried tae howld her ticht,
Wi' surprise, he cried 'O Maggie
    'E hev no goonie on 'e nicht.'

Geddes O'Mey 1978

TURKEY-COCK

You ruffled black blossom,
You glossy dark wind.

Your sort of gorgeousness,
Dark and lustrous
And skinny repulsive
And poppy-glossy,
Is the gorgeousness that evokes my most puzzled admiration.

Your aboriginality
Deep, unexplained,
Like a Red Indian darkly unfinished and aloof,
Seems like the black and glossy seeds of countless centuries.

Your wattles are the colour of steel-slag which has been red-hot
And is going cold,
Cooling to a powdery, pale-oxidised sky-blue.

Why do you have wattles, and a naked, wattled head?
Why do you arch your naked-set eye with a more-than-comprehensible arrogance!

The vulture is bald, so is the condor, obscenely,
But only you have thrown this amazing mantilla of oxidised sky-blue
And hot red over you.

This queer dross shawl of blue and vermilion,
Whereas the peacock has a diadem.

I wonder why.
Perhaps it is a sort of uncanny decoration, a veil of loose skin.
Perhaps it is your assertation, in all this ostentation, of raw contradictoriness.
Your wattles drip down like a shawl to your breast
And the point of your mantilla drops across your nose, unpleasantly.

Or perhaps it is something unfinished
A bit of slag still adhering, after your firing in the furnace of creation.

Or perhaps there is something in your wattles of a bull's dew-lap
Which slips down like a pendulum to balance the throbbing mass of a generous breast,
The over-drip of a great passion hanging in the balance.
Only yours would be a raw, unsmelted life, that will not quite fuse from the dross.

You contract yourself,
You arch yourself as an archer's bow
Which quivers indrawn as you clench your spine
Until your veiled head almost touches backward
To the root-rising of your erected tail.
And one intense and backward-curving frisson
Seizes you as you clench yourself together
Like some fierce magnet bringing its poles together.

Burning, pale positive pole of your wattled head!
And from the darkness of that opposite one
The upstart of your round-barred, sun-round tail!

Whilst between the two, along the tense arch of your back
Blows the magnetic current in fierce blasts,
Ruffling black, shining feathers like lifted mail,
Shuddering storm wind, or a water rushing through.
Your brittle super-sensual arrogance
Tosses the crape of red across your brow and down your breast
As you draw yourself upon yourself in insistence.

It is a declaration of such tension in will
As time has not dared to avouch, nor eternity been able to unbend
Do what it may.
A raw American will, that has never been tempered by life;
You brittle, will-tense bird with a foolish eye.

The peacock lifts his rods of bronze
And struts blue-brilliant out of the far East.
But watch a turkey prancing low on earth
Drumming his vaulted wings, as savages drum
Their rhythms on long-drawn, hollow, sinister drums.
The ponderous, sombre sound of the great drum of Huichilobos
In pyramid Mexico, during sacrifice.
Drum, and the turkey onrush,
Sudden, demonic dauntlessness, full abreast,
All the bronze gloss of all his myriad petals
Each one apart and instant.
Delicate frail crescent of the gentle outline of white
At each feather-tip
So delicate;
Yet the bronze wind-bell suddenly clashing
And the eye over-weening into madness.

Turkey-cock, turkey-cock
Are you the bird of the next dawn?
Has the peacock had his day, does he call in vain, screecher, for the sun to rise?
The eagle, the dove, and the barnyard rooster, do they call in vain, trying to wake the morrow?

And do you await us, wattled father, Westward?
Will your yell do it?

Take up the trail of the vanished American
Where it disappeared at the foot of the crucifix?
Take up the primordial Indian obstinacy,
The more than human, dense insistence of will,
And disdain, and blackness, and onrush, and prise open the new day with them?

The East a dead letter, and Europe moribund . . . Is that so?
And those sombre, dead, feather-lustrous Aztecs, Amerindians,
In all the sinister splendour of their red blood-sacrifices,
Do they stand under the dawn, half-godly, half-demon, awaiting the cry of the turkey-cock?

Or must you go through the fire once more, till you're smelted pure,
Slag-wattled turkey-cock,
Dross-jabot?

D. H. Lawrence (1885–1930)

MAY 7TH

By hiding behind a bush this morning – for they seem to have a great dislike of being watched – I saw a most curious form of courtship in progress between a cock and a hen turkey. They stood back to back at a little distance from each other, and then, after various deliberate preparations, began waltzing round in a circle, keeping their outspread tails pointing to each other. It reminded me of a figure in one of the square dances where the lady and gentleman walk round one another back to back.

Christmas tidings of good cheer
To turkeys seldom sound sincere.

Anon.

from *A Farmer's Year*, 1899
Rider Haggard (1856–1925)

The land girl and the milk maid

The milk maid was photographed by Sutcliffe in Whitby, Yorkshire between 1900–10; and the land girl was photographed by an unknown photographer about 1914. Although probably no more than five years separated the two photographs, it is interesting to note that the land girl was obviously a town girl working in the country for the period of the emergency, and very much a girl of the twentieth century, whereas the milk maid might have appeared the same a hundred years before.

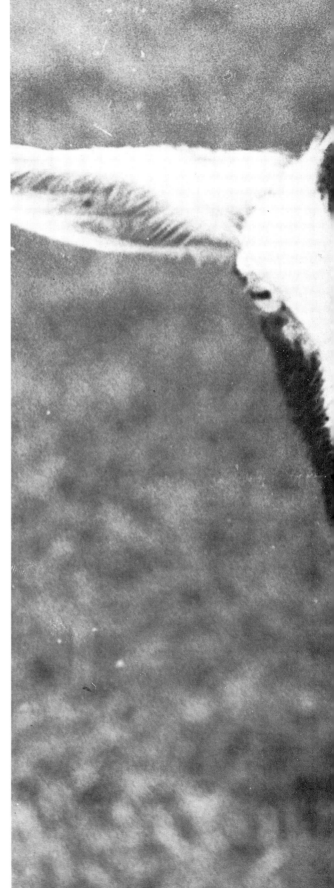

THE GOAT

The Billy goat's a handsome gent
But has a most far-reaching scent.
The Nanny goat is quite a belle.
Let's hope she has no sense of smell.

Roland Young

MY GOAT TINKER BELL, *TAKEN FROM*
JOURNEYS: PROSE BY CHILDREN OF THE
ENGLISH SPEAKING WORLD

She lies on the hay and I lie on her.
The rain drips off the roof while the rain
pours outside she's warm and I like just
lying there talking to her softly. It's
only a small shed about four feet high and
we're both squashed together but it's nice
just how I like to feel.

Susan Street, age 12, New Zealand

If Kids leap or stand upright, or gather
together in flocks or heards, and feed neer
together, it presageth Rain.

Prognosticks, 1669, **John Worlidge**

Boy scouts helping with the flax harvest,
August 1918.

Quoth a cow in the marshes of Glynn
All the world is divine, even sin.
As a natural creature
I worship all nature,
But most when the bullrush is in.

Conrad Aiken (1889–1973)

Why did the cow look over the wall?
Because it couldn't look through it.

Why does a pigeon roost on one leg?
*Because if he lifted the other he would
fall down.*

What makes more noise than a pig under a gate?
Two pigs under a gate.

Why do black sheep eat less than white sheep?
Because there are fewer of them.

If a cockerel lost his knees, what would he do?
*He would go to London because that's where
Cockneys are.*

When is a cow not a cow?
When it is turned into a field.

Why did the cowslip?
Because it saw the bulrush.

What did the big goat say to the little goat?
You can't kid me.

Why did the chicken cross the road?
Because it wanted to get to the other side.

What did the chicken say when it came
out of the egg?
Marmalade (Ma me laid).

There is a happy land, far, far, away,
Where little piggies run three times a day.
Oh! how they squeal and run,
When they hear the butcher come,
Three slices off their bum, three times a day.

Horse, pig, dog, goat,
You stink, I don't.

The cock, the hen, and the pullet,
Went into the barn to lay.
The cock and the hen came out again,
And which do you think did lay?

Mary had a little lamb
Its feet were black as soot
And onto Mary's bread and jam
Its sooty foot it put.
Now Mary was a careful child
Avoided every sham

She said – one little word that meant
The mother of that lamb.

Mary had a little lamb
With which she used to tussle
She pulled the wool from off its back
And stuffed it in her bustle.

Mary had a little lamb
Her father shot it dead
And now it goes to school with her
Between two chunks of bread.

Mary had a little lamb
With coat as black as soot
And into Mary's cup of milk
It put its dirty foot.
Now Mary, a straightforward girl,
Who hated any sham
Rapped out a naughty little word,
That rhymed with Mary's lamb.

Mary had a little lamb
It was a greedy glutton
She fed it on ice cream all day
And now it's frozen mutton.

Mary had a little lamb
She fed it castor oil
And everywhere the lamb would go
It fertilised the soil.

Mary had a little cow
It fed on safety pins
And every time she milked the cow
The milk came out in tins.

from *The Lore and Language of
Schoolchildren*, 1959
Iona and **Peter Opie**

Before the days of hay baling, all hay was piled in a hay stack, and because of the weight, the hay became tightly packed. It was necessary to slice it from the stack as required. This picture was taken in the 1930s.

134

A COW'S LIFE

It is no fond desire of mine
To wish that I'd been born bovine.
For cows must have a sad existence
Forever searching for subsistence.
They are just concubines, poor things
No marriage lines nor wedding rings
The only ring that is about
Is decorating Father's snout,
No birth control has been compiled
To stop that dreary annual child,
And if they love it (as they do)
It's wrestled from them P.D.Q.
The milk bar's flow (to put it crudely)
Is stolen from them very rudely.
Their horns are just reduced to stumps,
And red-hot irons upon their rumps

Impress some very painful sears,
While labels dangle from their ears.
Mixed bathing is a weekly torture
In most unpleasant smelling water.
Nebuchadnezzar once did try
To emulate their dietry
But soon he got as sick as mud
Of chewing, chewing at the cud.
So, surely they must sometimes wish
To have a slightly different dish,
A souffle, or meringues maybe
Instead of endless greenery?
And after having calves non-stop
They end up in the butcher's shop.
And so it really seems to me
A cow is NOT the thing to be.

Phyllis Haynes, 1980

135

In Ireland until the 1960's, the donkey was
by far the most used beast of burden.

Asses are used in many parts of the country for
carrying burdens, and have been lately introduced as farmers' stock: at Lord Moira's two or
three are constantly kept for carrying turnips,
cabbages, or other green food, for the supply of
live stock; they are worked by boys, or super-
annuated old men, or by women, and are perhaps,
the best stock that can be employed for clearing
green crops from strong land in wet weather;
their step being light, and not poaching the land;
they will easily carry two hundred weight; and an
ass has been known to carry 40 bricks, of 8 lb.
each, as its common burden, and will thus do a
great deal of work by perseverance, with the
assistance of those who are too weak to manage
horses. Some have the paniers constructed to
open at the bottom, to let out a load of turnips at
once, spreading them afterwards; and this stock is
approved by all who use them.

from *General View of the Agriculture of the
County of Leicester*,
William Pitt (1759–1806)

Donkey, donkey, old and grey,
Open your mouth and gently bray;
Lift your ears and blow your horn
To wake the world this sleepy morn.

Anon.

THE DONKEY

When fishes flew and forests walk'd
  And figs grew upon thorn,
Some moment when the moon was blood
  Then surely I was born;

With monstrous head and sickening cry
  And ears like errant wings,
The devil's walking parody
  On all four-footed things.

The tatter'd outlaw of the earth,
  Of ancient crooked will;
Starve, scourge, deride me: I am dumb,
  I keep my secret still.

Fools! For I also had my hour;
  One far fierce hour and sweet:
There was a shout about my ears,
  And palms before my feet.

              G. K. Chesterton (1872–1936)

INWARDLY FAT

An old chap in the village had a donkey, which
was very thin. On the road one day he was
stopped by a gentleman who said:
    'My man, your donkey is very thin.'
    'No Sar,' the old chap replied, 'it's
inwardly fat and the fat is pushing the bones
out.'

              William English, 1978

If the Ass bray more than ordinary, or without
any other apparent cause, it presageth Rain.

              Prognosticks, 1669, **John Worlidge**

The day Rosie Burdock decided to take me in hand was a motionless day of summer, creamy, hazy, and amber-coloured, with the beech trees standing in heavy sunlight as though clogged with wild wet honey. It was the time of haymaking, so when we came out of school Jack and I went to the farm to help.

The whirr of the mower met us across the stubble, rabbits jumped like firecrackers about the fields, and the hay smelt crisp and sweet. The farmer's men were all hard at work, raking, turning, and loading. Tall, whiskered fellows forked the grass, their chests like bramble patches. The air swung with their forks and the swathes took wing and rose like eagles to the tops of the wagons. The farmer gave us a short fork each and we both pitched in with the rest ...

I stumbled on Rosie behind a haycock, and she grinned up at me with the sly, glittering eyes of her mother. She wore her tartan frock and cheap brass necklace, and her bare legs were brown with hay-dust.

'Get out a there,' I said. 'Go on.'

Rosie had grown and was hefty now, and I was terrified of her. In her cat-like eyes and curling mouth I saw unnatural wisdoms more threatening than anything I could imagine. The last time we'd met I'd hit her with a cabbage stump. She bore me no grudge, just grinned.

'I got sommat to show ya.'

'You push off,' I said.

I felt dry and dripping, icy hot. Her eyes glinted, and I stood rooted. Her face was wrapped in a pulsating haze and her body seemed to flicker with lightning.

'You thirsty?' she said.

'I ain't, so there.'

'You be,' she said. 'C'mon.'

So I stuck the fork into the ringing ground and followed her, like doom.

We went a long way, to the bottom of the field, where a wagon stood half-loaded. Festoons of untrimmed grass hung down like curtains all around it. We crawled underneath, between the wheels, into a herb-scented cave of darkness. Rosie scratched about, turned over a sack, and revealed a stone jar of cider.

'It's cider,' she said. 'You ain't to drink it though. Not much of it, any rate.'

Huge and squat, the jar lay on the grass like an unexploded bomb. We lifted it up, unscrewed the stopper, and smelt the whiff of fermented apples. I held the jar to my mouth and rolled my eyes sideways, like a beast at a water-hole. 'Go on,' said Rosie. I took a deep breath ...

Never to be forgotten, that first long secret drink of golden fire, juice of those valleys and of that time, wine of wild orchards, of russet summer, of plump red apples, and Rosie's burning cheeks. Never to be forgotten, or ever tasted again ...

I put down the jar with a gulp and a gasp. Then I turned to look at Rosie. She was yellow and dusty with buttercups and seemed to be purring in the gloom; her hair was rich as a wild bee's nest and her eyes were full of stings. I did not know what to do about her, nor did I know what not to do. She looked smooth and precious, a thing of unplumbable mysteries, and perilous as quick-sand.

'Rosie ...' I said, on my knees, and shaking.

She crawled with a rustle of grass towards me, quick and superbly assured. Her hand in mine was like a small wet flame which I could neither hold nor throw away. Then Rosie, with a remorseless, reedy strength, pulled me down from my tottering perch, pulled me down, down into her wide green smile and into the deep subaqueous grass.

Then I remember little, and that little, vaguely. Skin drums beat in my head. Rosie was close-up, salty, an invisible touch, too near to be seen or measured. And it seemed that the wagon under which we lay went floating away like a barge, out over the valley where we rocked unseen, swinging on motionless tides.

Then she took off her boots and stuffed them with flowers. She did the same with mine. Her parched voice crackled like flames in my ears. More fires were started. I drank more cider. Rosie told me outrageous fantasies. She liked me, she said, better than Walt, or Ken, Boney Harris, or even the curate. And I admitted to her, in a loud, rough voice, that she was even prettier than Betty Gleed. For a long time we sat with our mouths very close, breathing the same hot air. We kissed, once only, so dry, and shy, it was like two leaves colliding in air.

At last the cuckoos stopped singing and slid into the woods. The mowers went home and left us. I heard Jack calling as he went down the lane, calling my name till I heard him no more. And still we lay in our wagon of grass tugging at each other's hands, while her husky, perilous whisper drugged me and the cider beat gongs in my head ...

Night came at last, and we crawled out from the wagon and stumbled together towards home. Bright dew and glow-worms shone over the grass, and the heat of the day grew softer. I felt like a giant; I swung from the trees and plunged my arms into nettles just to show her. Whatever I did seemed valiant and easy. Rosie carried her boots, and smiled.

from *Cider with Rosie*
Laurie Lee (1914–   )

This photograph of a team making a hay rick
was taken circa 1900 by John Henry Knight,
pioneer motorist and early photographer. Note
the elevator driven by the horse and the rolled
tent above the hay rick waiting to be let down to
protect the rick from the weather until thatching.

The last days of my childhood were also the last days of the village. I belonged to that generation which saw, by chance, the end of a thousand years' life. The change came late to our Cotswold valley, didn't really show itself till the late 1920s; I was twelve by then, but during that handful of years I witnessed the whole thing happen.

Myself, my family, my generation, were born in a world of silence; a world of hard work and necessary patience, of backs bent to the ground, hands massaging crops, of waiting on weather and growth; of villages like ships in the empty landscapes and the long walking distances between them; of white narrow roads, rutted by hooves and cartwheels, innocent of oil or petrol, down which people passed rarely, and almost never for pleasure, and the horse was the fastest thing moving. Man and horse were all the power we had – abetted by levers and pulleys. But the horse was king, and almost everything grew around him: fodder, smithies, stables, paddocks, distances, and the rhythm of our days. His eight miles an hour was the limit of our movements, as it had been since the days of the Romans. That eight miles and hour was life and death, the size of our world, our prison.

from *Cider with Rosie*
Laurie Lee (1914–   )

This 'one off' tractor built by Henry Ford was soon to be followed in 1917 by the first mass-produced Ford tractors. More than anything else, the tractor has been responsible for the changes in the English countryside and the disappearance of the working horse. As tractors and other mechanised vehicles have become larger, the landscape has been forced to change, causing narrow lanes and hedges to disappear, and small fields to be merged.

This picture was taken in March 1918.
I wonder what they were all really thinking

It was not until the First World War that a reversal of the labour drift from the land to the towns took place. Women from all walks of life came to the land as members of the Women's Land Army. At first they were laughed at, but although their numbers were small they commanded considerable respect by the end of the war. When hostilities again flared in 1939, a gigantic well-organised land army of women was mobilised and thousands of men were released to defend their country. For the first time in history, when hostilities had ceased and the girls returned to town life, the farming community felt that it had an army of ambassadresses well-qualified to defend and explain the position of farm people and farm life.

*The Land Army arrives. A scene near the
Lancashire Institute of Agriculture outside
Preston where many of the land girls were
trained – November 1939.*

top left: Elsa Buchanan, an up and coming British actress of the late thirties, was one of the first members of the Women's Land Army in 1939.

top right: Doreen Munns must have been the prettiest rat catcher that Hereford County Council ever employed.

bottom left: Daphne Vincent continues her tractor driving during a doodle-bug (flying bomb) raid, July 1944.

bottom right: Not surprisingly, this land girl was a trapeze artist before she joined up.

top: 1939: an unwilling subject. The girl wanted to
go milking, but the cow had other ideas.

bottom: This land girl receives her proficiency badge
not altogether admired by her onlooker.

February 23rd, 1944: *Punch*

"I haven't seen a fillet steak for years," complains a London correspondent. If he could snatch a week-end in the country he would see plenty, as well as rump, point and chateaubriand. And off-the-ration oxtails, too.

April 11th, 1945: *Punch*

30th June, 1970: *Daily Mirror*

" HE CAN'T DECIDE WHETHER TO PLOUGH AND SOW AND REAP AND MOW OR JUST ORGANISE A 120 ACRE POP FESTIVAL."

150

HAPPY CALF

Mother is worried, her low, short moos
Question what's going on. But her calf
Is quite happy, resting on his elbows,
With his wrists folded under, and his precious hind legs
Brought up beside him, his little hooves
Of hardly-used yellow-soled black.
She looms up, to reassure him with heavy lickings.
He wishes she'd go away. He's meditating
Black as a mole and as velvety,
With a white face-mask, and a pink parting,
With black tear-patches, but long
Glamorous white eyelashes. A mild narrowing
Of his eyes, as he lies, testing each breath
For its peculiar flavour of being alive.
Such a pink muzzle, but a black dap
Where he just touched his mother's blackness
With a tentative sniff. He is all quiet
While his mother worries to and fro, grazes a little,
Then looks back, a shapely mass
Against the South sky and the low frieze of hills,
And moos questioning warning. He just stays,
Head slightly tilted, in the mild illness
Of being quite contented, and patient
With all the busyness inside him, the growing
Getting under way. The wind from the North
Marching the high silvery floor of clouds
Trembles the grass-stalks near him. His head wobbles
Infinitesimally in the pulse of his life.
A buttercup leans on his velvet hip.
He folds his head back little by breathed little
Till it rests on his shoulder, his nose on his ankle,
And he sleeps. Only his ears stay awake.

from *Moortown*, 1979
Ted Hughes

Hay making at Cartmel in the Lake District
in the 1930s.

JERUSALEM

And did those feet in ancient time
   Walk upon England's mountains green?
And was the holy lamb of God
   On England's pleasant pastures seen?

And did the Countenance Divine
   Shine forth upon our clouded hills?
And was Jerusalem builded here
   Among these dark Satanic Mills?

Bring me my bow of burning gold!
   Bring me my arrows of desire!
Bring me my spear! O clouds, unfold!
   Bring me my chariot of fire!

I will not cease from mental fight,
   Nor shall my sword sleep in my hand,
Till we have built Jerusalem
   In England's green and pleasant land.

William Blake (1757–1827)

The Crook family have lived at Blue House
Farm, Little London, Suffolk (all of five houses),
since the main house was originally built in the
sixteenth century. Howard Crook farms 200
acres, and his livestock includes pigs, sheep,
turkeys, ducks, guinea fowl, bantams, geese,.
chickens and a goat. As on all real farms, the
whole family is involved.

All of these animals have existed on British farms this century. How many will our grandchildren see?

PIGS
Lincolnshire Curly
Tamworth
Middle White
Berkshire
Gloucester Old Spot
British Lop
Large Black
British Saddleback
Oxford Sandy and Black
Old Berkshire
Hampshire
Saddleback
Large White
Welsh
British Landrace

CATTLE
Irish Dun
Suffolk Dun
Alderney
Fifeshire
Light Park
Kerry
Jersey
Shetland
Northern Dairy Shorthorn
Dexter
Red Pole
White Gallaway
Belted Gallaway
Bolian Gwynion
Blue Albion
Charrolais
Guernsey
Sussex
Devon
Hereford
Aberdeen Angus
Scottish Highland
Ayrshire
Norfolk Red Pole

SHEEP
Portland
Manx Loghtan
Wensleydale
Leicester Long Wool
Cotswold
White Faced Woodland
Oxford Down
Ryland
Teeswater
Shropshire
Lleyn
North Ronaldsway
Soay
Hebridean
Wiltshire Horn
Shetland
South Down
Black Welsh Mountain
Jacob
New Norfolk Horn
Suffolk
Castlemilk Shetland
Cheviot
Romany
Hampshire
Berkshire

HORSES
Exmoor Pony
Caspian
Suffolk Punch
Dales Pony
Fell Pony
Dartmoor
Shire
Clydesdale
British Percheron
Cleveland Bay
Welsh Cob
Welsh Mountain Pony

CHICKENS
Lanshan
Orpington
Leghorn
Minorca
Brahma-Dorking
Hamburg
Creve-Cours
Rhode Island Red
Arbor Acre
Cochin
Light Sussex
North Holland Blue
Marans
Rocks
Faverolles
Malines
Scots Dumpy
Silkie
Wyandottes
Bresse
Anconas
Houdans

DUCKS
Aylesbury
Pekin
Rouen
Khaki Campbell
Welsh Harlequin
White Campbell
Dark Campbell
Indian Runner

GEESE
Embden
Toulouse
Brecon Buff
Chinese
Roman

TURKEYS
Broad Breasted White
Broad Breasted Bronze
Norfolk Black
Norfolk White

A pig fattening unit

A Basingstoke egg production unit

ACKNOWLEDGEMENTS

The illustrations in this book appear by courtesy of the following:

Bowes Museum, 59, 88, 94, 96, 98, 120;

British Farmer and Stockbreeder, 156, 157;

BBC Hulton Picture Library, 3, 129, 132, 144, 146, 147;

British Library, 8, 17, 19, 31;

Mr A. Dent, St. Pierre-de-Chignac, France, 28;

Mary Evans Picture Library, 14, 15, 36, 40, 42, 43, 48, 54, 58, 59, 69, 70, 71, 73, 74, 75, 76, 80, 91, 97, 134;

Farnham Museum, 140/1;

Ford Motor Company, 143;

Fox Photos Ltd., 145, 146, 147;

Institute of Agricultural History and Museum of English Rural Life, University of Reading, 20, 45, 56, 66/7, 72, 77, 78, 79, 89, 101, 122, 135;

Museum of Lakeland Life and Industry, Abbot Hall, Kendal, 89, 152/3 – Joseph Hardman, 82, 83, 103 – attributed to Walmsley Bros.;

National Library of Ireland, 64, 65;

Punch, 63, 68, 148, 149;

Suffolk Record Office, 84/5, 87, 99, 104, 105, 108/9, 110/1, 117;

Sutcliffe Gallery, 119, 128;

Ulster Folk and Transport Museum, 136;

Victoria and Albert Museum, Crown Copyright, 12, 13, 24/5, 52/3;

Keith Waite, 149.

The following photographs were taken by Peter Isaac: 1, 6, 39, 60, 61, 86, 100, 107, 112, 113, 114, 115, 116, 123, 125, 127, 131, 150, 154, 158.

Copyright poems and passages of prose appear courtesy of the following:

Conrad Aiken: the Estate of the late Conrad Aiken, Copyright © 1963, 1964 by Conrad Aiken;

Geoffrey Chaucer: from *The Nun's Priest's Tale* by Chaucer from Chaucer: THE CANTERBURY TALES, trans. Nevill Coghill (Penguin Classics, Revised edition, 1977) p. 233, Copyright © Nevill Coghill, 1958, 1960, 1975, 1977, reprinted by permission of Penguin Books Ltd.;

G.K. Chesterton: the Estate of G.K. Chesterton and J.M. Dent & Sons Ltd.;

Simon Dewes: *A Suffolk Childhood* published by Hutchinson General Books Ltd.;

James Hawker: *James Hawker's Journal: A Victorian Poacher*, © Oxford University Press 1961, by permission of Oxford University Press;

Ted Hughes: reprinted by permission of Faber and Faber Ltd. from *Moortown* by Ted Hughes;

D.H. Lawrence: Laurence Pollinger Ltd. and the Estate of the late Mrs Frieda Lawrence Ravagli, from *The Complete Poems of D.H. Lawrence* published by William Heinemann Ltd.;

Laurie Lee: The Hogarth Press, from *Cider with Rosie* by Laurie Lee;

Iona and Peter Opie: from *The Lore and Language of Schoolchildren* by Iona and Peter Opie (1955), reprinted by permission of Oxford University Press;

Jack Prelutsky: *Zoo Doings* by Jack Prelutsky, published by Hamish Hamilton Ltd.;

Laurens van der Post: from *The Heart of the Hunter* by Laurens van der Post, The Hogarth Press and William Morrow and Company Inc. Thanks also to Mrs Phyllis Haynes, Mr William English and Mr Geddes O'Mey for their kind contributions.

I began to think if there were
no such place as London
it really would be very desirable
to live in the country.

Sir Arthur Helps (1813–75)